ONLY
STRANGERS
TRAVEL

ONLY STRANGERS TRAVEL

SHARON HAWKINSON

Bookcraft
Salt Lake City, Utah

Library of Congress Catalog Card Number: 84-71069
ISBN 0-88494-533-2

First Printing, 1984

Lithographed in the United States of America
PUBLISHERS PRESS
Salt Lake City, Utah

To Karon

Contents

Brown Shoes

The man at the pulpit paused for a long moment, squeezing his eyes into narrow slits.

"Everyone here today will die," he said as he jabbed his forefinger in the direction of the deacons, then back again toward the ward clerk. "And everyone here will be resurrected. Not one person in this room will get out of going through that experience."

He paused again, his left hand holding the podium as if to keep it from flying away. Then his mouth closed tight, and he gazed into the corners of the chapel as if he were watching each of us solemnly marching to our coffins. The other kids on the bench beside me squirmed in his harsh silence, but I was mesmerized. I'd never thought about death before, and suddenly I saw myself walking through death's door, wearing a lacy white dress and flowing gauze veil, to stand in the blinding gold of the resurrection. How fortunate for us that we could all die—how wonderful!

For days after, I dreamt about dying. I decided I wanted Evan Miller to sing "I Am a Child of God" at my funeral, and my grandfather—because he loved me the most and would be sure to say the best things—to talk. I would lie serene and smiling in my pink satin-lined coffin as if I had just fallen asleep, and everyone would whisper and sigh over how pretty I looked and over what a shame it was. I, of course, would stay around in my spirit body, hovering somewhere in the back of the chapel before floating off to heaven. After all, it was my finale.

Death fascinated me, intrigued me, and everywhere I turned, people seemed to be talking about it—especially older people—like children playing hospital or like mothers smoothing wrinkles out of dresses. I read obituaries in the newspaper every night and fervently wished someone I knew would die so I could attend my first funeral.

Then I caught the Asian flu, and I wished I were dead as I lay on the cool bathroom floor between vomitings. I was sick a long time, and Mother finally packed me off to my grandparents to get more rest. For many days I lay on a couch watching fragmented sunlight slide over the furniture and listening to chopped-up conversation. My head felt lumpy and the churning in my stomach often swirled up to slam against my ears, causing two pounding spots above my eyes. My tongue felt thick and sour. But soon, although pale and weak, I was able to work on my lessons and go to the store with my grandmother. Things were still a little out of focus, but I remember health slowly filling my body again like rain dripping into an empty bucket.

One winter night my grandfather wrapped me in a blanket, and we drove into the country to visit relatives. Snow was blowing across the road like thin foam. After passing many sectioned-off fields covered with cold moonlight (I started counting them), we turned down a rutted lane to an old cabin that seemed to lean against some pine trees like a tired man slumping against his barn. Its corners were uneven as if a giant hand had crumpled it and tossed it against the trees.

"I sure don't feel much like visiting," my grandmother complained as she stepped into the snow.

"I know, but it's got to be done. No use stewing about it. Lizzy's so sick, this'll probably be the last chance we'll have to see her this side of heaven."

"Well, if she's so sick she probably doesn't want any company," my grandmother snapped.

I hung back from climbing out of the car and looked up at the windows. A real dying lady was behind them—someone whose turn to step through the veil was very close.

"What's she got?" I asked my grandfather.

"Who?"

"The lady who's almost dead—what's she got, flu?"

One side of my grandfather's face jerked, but quickly fell back into the hard lines around his mouth. "She hasn't got anything. She's just dying."

"Oh."

He knocked loudly (at least it seemed loud to me if there was someone dying on the other side), while Grandmother still sputtered quietly to the snow behind us, as if she wanted each ice crystal to understand why we shouldn't go visiting on a winter's night.

When a small, frowning woman opened the door, light poured out like thick soup, covering us and the snow with a yellow tint. I was surprised by the inside of the cabin. It was poorer—but cleaner— than any place I'd ever seen. Old linoleum shone in the light from a rock fireplace, and a picture of the Idaho Falls Temple hung high on rose-covered wallpaper. In front of a small window was a long couch with deep shaggy cushions on which sat two girls wearing heavy sweaters and skirts. Across the room stood a single-burner cooking stove with a pipe running up through the ceiling, and next to it sat the dying lady. I knew she was the one. Wrapped in a blue shawl, she rocked slowly back and forth with her hands resting on the sides of the rocker. She was very old. Her mouth folded accordion style, and the skin on her hands rolled into deep gulleys. On one finger she wore a small pearl ring, but her knuckles were so swollen I wondered how she ever got it off.

Just then a rosy-cheeked man—hard all over from plenty of outside work—and two tall boys spilled into the room from a side doorway. I wondered how so many could live in such a small room. Like dogs in a kennel, they all seemed to be moving on top of each other. The twinkling man alone could have filled up the whole house with his animal energy.

"Well, look at who's come to visit: Frank Morgan, you ol' son-of-a-gun." The man grabbed at my grandfather's hand and slapped his back at the same time. "Dessie?" he nodded to my grandmother. "How are ya? Sit, sit. Girls, get some of that rhubarb pie in here and make some hot chocolate." The two girls reluctantly unfolded themselves from the couch.

"No, no thanks, Lloyd. We just come for a minute— didn't catch ya at your chores, did we?"

"Naw, just finished. Get it anyway, girls. Colder than a dog's nose out there tonight, ain't it?" He turned to the old lady. *"Mother, look at who's come to see you."* He accented the words heavily, then said in a softer voice, "She ain't so good. Ever since Dad died, we can't seem to get the cold out of her bones." He leaned over her again. *"Mother."*

"I heard ya, Lloyd." Raising her eyelids slowly as if they weighed too much, she looked at my grandfather. "Frank," she nodded.

"How are ya, Liz?"

"Well, I've sure been better—got too many pains to be feeling real good."

"Now, now, Mother," boomed the twinkling man in a voice you use to shush small children. "Don't listen to her, she's just doing fine, just fine."

The old woman didn't say anything, although I saw something sharp flick in her eyes. She just settled quietly back into her rocking.

The twinkling man wanted me to go into the kitchen with his girls, but I slid down by my grandmother's feet onto a rug in front of the stove. Heat crept up my arms as I studied the old woman's shoes. She never stopped rocking. Every now and then she'd raise her eyes as if she recognized a name or place the others were discussing, but then she'd slide back into her own thoughts again as if their talk was too small to bother with. Her eyes seemed to be watching something big and unending like a heavy, gray rolling sea. But soon they shifted to my grandmother's face. "Hello, Dessie," she said quietly, making the others stop talking for a moment.

I liked her. She seemed worn and tired and sort of loose like a snapped rubber band, but she also seemed lovely, like lazy dust particles floating in afternoon sunlight. She made me think of a blue Chinese vase I had seen in a curio shop— strong lines, delicate, and simple. As I watched the old woman rock, small pockets of turbulence settled inside me, and the heat from the stove seeped under my skin to lick at bones and muscle. I felt almost hypnotized, as if I were melting into my grandmother's leg.

Once, the dying lady looked at me. Her lips didn't move, but a soft smile filled her eyes as she studied my face and hair. We gazed at each other as if we were holding hands, though it would have been unthinkable to touch. Our sickness separated us from the others, raised us above and away to a cushioned silence. I was in a strange place and so was she—some foreign, fuzzy landscape. Someday I wanted to come back here and talk to her—but not now, not tonight. It was enough to sit near her calm rocking.

I woke up as my grandfather put me into the back seat. It was bitter cold, and snow was blowing hard now. My grandfather was reminding Grandmother that he had to get up at four to take some women to the temple in Idaho Falls, and wouldn't it have been wiser to have left an hour ago.

"Well, I don't care," said my grandmother, gathering steam. "It done her good to visit with us. Death is just sitting there in her face, and she don't have long for this world. Course, they say that death's just a step through the veil and tastes sweet to the righteous, and there's none been more

righteous than Lizzy. I don't think she's missed paying her
tithing once in her whole life, and I don't know nobody
kinder.''

Just then a black cat ran across the road and Grandmother
told Gramps to stop right now and turn around and go back
to the crossroads. Grandfather said it was another ten miles
extra to go that way home, and besides in the moonlight he
thought he'd seen that the cat had a white paw. Grandmother
said there wasn't no moon and she didn't trust black cats and
they weren't going to chance it, especially with one of the
grandchildren with them. Gramps told her the snow was
going to turn into a full blizzard any minute. But Grandmother folded her arms and shook her head and said she'd
get out right now and walk home rather than drive on another inch. Didn't he remember what happened to Elsie last
summer after that black cat had crossed her path?

Finally Grandfather looked at her long and hard, then
shook his head, chuckling, and we drove the ten miles out of
our way home to a warm kitchen. The next morning before
light, I heard the car warming up in the driveway as he got
ready for the temple. Grandmother stayed home and spent
the afternoon teaching me how to crochet.

My grandfather was a big man, strong, and sure of himself.
A couple of weeks later he took me to buy new shoes, and I
felt proud walking beside him. Inside the store I tried on
some pretty, shiny black pumps I'd seen in the window, with
taps on the heels, but Grandfather asked the saleslady to
bring out some heavier, brown shoes. I held my breath for
the shiny pumps, even though they pinched my toes slightly,
but Grandfather said the brown ones were more practical and
sturdy.

As we left the store and walked to the barbershop, I felt as
though the people we passed were secretly glancing at my
feet and thinking ''she's wearing new shoes.'' At the barber's I
listened to him drone out of the side of his mouth and swung
my legs back and forth, studying the brown shoes. I guessed
they were not so bad; they'd be nice to run in, but they sure

were too cloppy and heavy to wear with a dress. I had sensed we were going somewhere important that afternoon, since Grandmother had curled my hair in little white rags last night, and I hoped they wouldn't make me wear the brown shoes with a dress.

But they did. They made me wear those ugly brown shoes to my first funeral. Two hours later, curled and scrubbed, we pulled in front of a building called Ekerson's Funeral Home. As we climbed out of the car to follow others, dressed in Sunday-best, moving slowly in front of us, I wondered why they called it a "home." Did someone live here?

Inside, everything—from floor to ceiling—was red velvet. Heavy oak chairs stood empty, and a sweet smell like old potatoes pushed against my face. A man wearing a dark suit and a very white shirt was shaking hands, speaking softly to people who were passing through heavy drapes into organ music.

"Sorry to greet you on such a sad occasion, Frank."

"Well, Harold, I figure it's for the best. This here is my granddaughter."

"Hello, young lady. My, you've sure grown up fast." As he shook my hand he was pulling me into the room.

"They certainly grow up fast, don't they, Dessie?"

"Yes, yes, too fast; life passes too quickly, Harold."

We slid along a wooden pew to the wall where more red drapes hung as the organ lady began to play "O My Father." I tucked my feet way back under the bench so no one could see the brown shoes. After sitting quietly for a moment Grandmother said, "Well, I guess I better go up and pay my last respects." Then she rustled up the aisle with the others, passing some ladies who were coming back holding Kleenexes to their noses.

"Where's she going?" I whispered to Grandfather.

"Up to view the body. You can go with her if you want."

No, I couldn't, not with the brown shoes on. I wanted to, but I just couldn't. I studied the wood grain on the back of the pew and the lady's fur hat in front of us. Soon the organ lady started another hymn, and I noticed fewer people were walking up the aisle. Most sat with bowed heads. *Maybe I could sneak up to the coffin unnoticed now,* I thought, as Grandmother settled down beside me.

"May I go look, Grandmother?"

"Well, hurry, they're about to start."

Tiptoeing slowly towards the cream-colored coffin, wanting to just peek over the side for a moment, I edged closer, tingling all over as if I were going to catch a butterfly. But suddenly I stiffened. My shoes dug hard into the red carpet, and my legs felt like lead. The corpse was Lizzy, my dying lady. Anyway it looked like her. No, it wasn't. Moving forward now as if pulled by a rope, I raised my hand to brush aside something cold and crawly that seemed to touch my skin. She wore the pearl ring; it was her, but she looked so straight and cold—colder than the snowiest night. Her lips, cakey and thin, were pursed as though she were about to kiss someone she didn't like. Her eyes were closed, but not softly, more as if someone's thumb had pushed them down hard into clay cheeks. Around her face a white veil fluffed, making her skin look grey. Swollen hands crossed over a lacy white dress looking as if they'd break like peanut brittle if I picked one up.

Saliva oozed up from the back of my throat, and I wanted to spit. Then behind me someone whispered, "She looks peaceful."

"Yes, they did a good job on her, didn't they?"

I thought Lizzy looked as if someone had beaten her with a rolling pin, then tried to cover it up with dabs of white powder and rouge. The sweet smell rose up around me, filling my mouth and nose, and I backed away from the coffin as if it were reaching out for me. Then I felt a big hand squeezing my shoulder and glanced up to see my grandfather staring at Lizzy, too. He stood silent, then looked down at me. His eyes softened, and somehow I knew he understood how sick I felt. He motioned with his head for us to go back, holding my hand now down the aisle.

As I crawled over next to my grandmother, who patted my knee, the organ lady stopped playing hymns and a partially bald man got up to offer the prayer.

"We know, O Lord, that death is sweet to the righteous. Help those of us who are left behind to understand that and feel comforted."

With my arms folded and head bowed, I studied my shoes again under half-closed eyes. Even though I'd been careful, they were already caked with mud. I had really needed new shoes. My old ones had been falling apart at the seams and didn't fit anymore.

Another man in a too-tight suit rose to speak. His face was sunburned up to the middle of his forehead, where it glistened white. He looked as if he wished he were milking cows.

"Elizabeth Martin was the kindest, sweetest person I know," he said with his mouth too far away from the microphone. "I remember one time when me and my family hit a rough spot. It was a worse winter than the one we got outside them doors right now. And Lizzy come with bread and milk and apple pie."

He spoke for seven minutes; I was watching the clock carefully. Then the bishop spoke, and their voices washed over me like sudsy water while I leaned against my grandfather's arm. I longed to escape the red curtains and get out into the winter air away from that stale smell. I swung my legs back and forth to the bishop's words, suddenly realizing that the brown shoes didn't seem so heavy anymore. When I got home my twin sister would envy me; she needed new shoes, too. *They aren't so bad,* I thought. *At least they don't pinch like the shiny black pumps did. And, after all, they are new. I'll get used to them soon.*

I learned I had to get used to a lot of things in life—even death. But for a long time death and dying scared me, like slow black seepage filled with leeches—especially spiritual death, where bodies continue to walk around long after something in the eyes has dimmed.

2

Traveling Fishermen

I was born in Rigby, Idaho, a small Mormon town just north of Idaho Falls, which is named after a cascading waterfall on the Snake River—the same Snake River that Lewis and Clark traveled. The Snake streams from the Teton Mountains in several different forks, feeding the valley below where Mormons and Gentiles farm wheat and potatoes.

My great-grandparents walked across the plains with other Mormon pioneers. Neither heroes nor fools, they were simply quiet farmers who wanted to farm—and to be left alone to live their peculiar religion. After Mormons reached the west, they worked hard to make the barren deserts of Utah, Arizona, and Idaho blossom like a rose and to raise righteous children unto the Lord. Babies fell from heaven into polygamous families like rain; just as the rain was a gift to the desert land, so were the children considered a sacred blessing and responsibility from the Lord.

My grandparents were both born in La Belle, Idaho, a sparse scattering of houses along the Snake just outside of Rigby. They became a watered-down version of my great-grandparents. I remember my grandfather as a curious mixture of devout Mormon, sensible farmer, and superstitious Welshman. As I was growing up, he developed back trouble and his wide chest slowly fell forward. My grandmother was named Deseret, the Book of Mormon word for honeybee. She was small, shy, and romantic, and not as religious as my grandfather. For many years she liked her coffee in the mornings, and I heard her swear a string of cuss words on more than one occasion. Her kitchen always smelled like raisin cookies. Every time we'd come for a visit, I'd race my sister across the back porch, where the old fruit cellar was, to the cookie jar. And I always won. We were allowed two cookies per visit.

My grandmother must have had about a million different knickknacks on her shelves. Smooth dogs with droopy ears, shiny cats, and shepherd boys and girls sat in prim rows watching each other with black and brown painted eyes. There was a small ballerina with a tiny painted face and a pink china skirt. Porcelain horses pranced or bucked or stood stiff-legged, ears pointed, heads high as if they smelled a storm in the wind. When we were little, Grandma let us take them down one by one and hold them. My favorites were the music boxes. A boy with loose blue pants swirled a china girl to tinny sounding music. She had her head turned and her eyes closed and a painted smile on her lips. Another small box played a marching song as a fat red clown pounded cymbals together.

Grandma's shelves were fairylands for us, but I'll never forget the afternoon that Karon dropped the white swan and its head broke off. (The tiny swan was the most prized of all the figurines because it was the oldest. Grandma's mother had given it to her when she was little.) Karon's face turned white, then bright red, and she didn't dare raise her eyes and look at Grandma's face. I looked, though, and I never wanted to hold any of the knickknacks again. After several seconds of silence, Grandma smoothed down Karon's hair and said, "Now, it was just an accident. Bring it into the kitchen, and I think we can glue it back together."

It was the custom in our family to send the children to spend different weekends with different relatives, so that they would grow up intimately acquainted with cousins, aunts and uncles, and especially grandparents. On many weekends my sister and I stayed with Grandma, who loved parading us in fluffed pink dresses past the neighbors at church on Sunday morning. On Saturday night we were scrubbed and dried with her softest towels; then she'd make us sit on a tall stool while she tied pieces of our long hair in white rags to make ringlets. After wrapping us in cotton nightgowns, she'd give us hot bread and tell us stories about our dad growing up and going off to war. She thought he was a grand person because he'd seen Korea and fought in the jungles.

Grandmother felt it her personal duty to make sure we knew our great-great-aunts and uncles, too, and on Sunday after church we'd visit their old rock homesteads along the river. One afternoon we drove down a dusty lane to a small, two-story house sitting on a slight hill. Two small boys a few years older than us were playing catch on an immaculate lawn, and on the porch a tall, dark woman stood in the shadow of the door, her arms crossed, her gray hair drawn back tightly in a small bun. She hugged my grandmother stiffly, awkwardly, before they moved into her cluttered kitchen. After we'd been properly fussed over, Grandma excused us to go out to play. We moved slowly down the hill in the direction of the two boys, pretending we didn't see them.

"Hey," the taller one yelled, "you wanna see something?" Karon looked at me and I shrugged, denying any curiosity that might nudge us into a trap. They motioned for us to follow as they crawled through a break in the white fence into thick grass and weeds taller than I was.

"Any snakes in there?" Karon asked.

"Sure," said the blond boy over his shoulder as he beat a path in front of him with a long stick. We followed slowly, untangling our Sunday dresses carefully now and then from thistles and sticker weeds. Soon we came to a patch of shorter grass, in the middle of which stood the biggest spreading tree I'd ever seen. Its branches reached upward across the sky and outward to hang over a broken-down wooden fence. Bees hummed around tiny blossoms surrounding the trunk, and I could see a bird's nest high up in the branches.

The blond boy swung himself up on a low limb and scrambled through green sun-speckled leaves; then he began throwing something down to the taller boy, who handed me two, round, soft, purple balls.

"Plums," he said as he popped one in his mouth. Juice ran down the left side of his chin, and he held his head forward to keep it from dripping on his shirt. "Try one."

It was a dare, a test, and we knew if we didn't bite into a plum, they'd leave us there to find our way back, calling us "City Slickers, City Slickers." I bit first, juice spraying out from all sides of my mouth, and I was surprised at how good they were. Karon bit gingerly into hers, pulling a face. "Sour."

The two boys stood behind the tree now, whispering behind their hands and shoving each other. Soon the blond one came walking over with his hands full of plums. We could hear the taller boy giggling. As the blond boy got close to Karon, he reached up and kissed her quickly on the cheek, then ran back to the taller boy. Both roared with laughter as they turned and jumped the fence, falling on the other side to roll in the tall grass, then running hard towards the barn, the fall barely breaking their stride. Karon threw her plums down and reached up to wipe her cheek in disgust. I was slightly horrified but giggled nervously, ready to leap like a deer towards the house if they came back.

On the way home Grandma wanted an explanation for how dirty and sticky we were.

"We ate plums from the plum tree in the garden."

"Is that plum tree still there?" She got a faraway look in her eyes and her face softened. "When I was a little girl I ate plums from that tree, too."

Because of Grandfather's back trouble he slept in the other room, where it was cold, with a heavy desk and dark brown wardrobe. In winter he always heated three hot water bottles for our feet before evening prayer, then Grandma would tuck us in beside her. Her sheets always smelled of gardenias. Before turning to the scriptures, she'd always read to us a little from a novel she had hid under her bed. The hot water bottle felt good against my feet as I snuggled down beside my sister, listening to the old house twisting and shuffling in the night.

Grandfather was up first on Sunday morning to stoke up the stove. By the time my sister and I had shivered into our bathrobes, ham would be frying and the kitchen windows steaming. Grandma would set the checkered tablecloth with plates of thick bread and ham, and apricot and peach preserves. They treated food with reverence.

My father once told me that this was because of the depression. Grandfather was forced to go as far away as Montana to find work, leaving Grandma behind with four children in a small cabin. She gleaned fields for food, laying the baby on a blanket under an apple tree and taking the three older ones to help her pick potatoes that the hired workers had missed.

One season she felt lucky to get a job picking apples. She'd always loved apple trees because as a young girl she'd spent hours in the spring strolling under clouds of apple blossoms, pink mushroom umbrellas, dreaming of wearing frothy dresses as fine as the blossoms. She imagined someday she'd be rich and live in San Francisco. But things didn't turn out like her dreams, and now she stood on ladders under apple trees, endlessly filling bushel after bushel for a few pennies a day. Needles crawled up her arms, and her back throbbed far into the night. Now she dreamed of getting eight hours of sleep and of putting enough food in front of her children.

But Grandfather would never let her whine. Things just had to be lived through. "Tomorrow it'll get better, Mom," he'd say, but it never did get too much better.

They weren't as bad off as their neighbors, though, because in a small shed behind the cabin stood a Brown-Swiss milk cow that gave out not only enough milk for the family but some extra to sell. However, one month, to buy long pants for my dad, Grandma used the cream that should have gone to pay tithing. It seems he was to be in a Primary program, and she was ashamed to have him stand in front of the neighbors wearing patched short pants. The next week Grandma found the cow in the field, bloated and stiff, and no one could convince her that she wasn't being punished by God for not paying tithing. She wept for days, and she never missed paying her tenth to the Church again.

Grandma always felt she was backward because she'd quit school in the eighth grade to work as a housemaid for a Catholic businessman in Idaho Falls. He was the only Catholic she had ever met in her whole life, and she made it a point to tell people what a gentleman he was and how—no matter what he believed in—he always treated her real fine. She kept his grand house in order, and in return she had a small salary and her own room above the kitchen with ruffled curtains at the window and flowered pillowcases. Later when my grandfather took his bride home to a small cabin along the Snake River, she could never get used to the dirt floor under the tick carpet. But my grandmother worked hard all her life to make things comfortable for my grandfather.

As the patriarch of his family in the true Mormon fashion, my grandfather made decisions quickly and cleanly as if he were shooting cans off a fence post. I remember my Aunt Theo telling me once how Grandfather had made my father and my uncle haul hay with a team of horses all night because they'd gone fishing instead of working in the fields while he had gone to town. About two o'clock in the morning it started to rain, and my uncle coaxed my dad into speaking to Grandfather about coming in. "Ask him. He likes you better than me." But as they drove the team by the house to the barn, they saw Grandfather leaning against the door, watching them, and neither spoke a word.

In the summer Grandma would make jars and jars of raspberry jam. She never felt they had enough food. On hot summer days, she'd stand for hours over huge, boiling kettles of fruit and vegetables, her sleeves rolled up and a hairnet covering her long red hair. She was always very careful to drop the peaches gently with the cut side down into hot sterilized jars, and she wanted the beans snapped just the right length. Then she'd have us kids shine the bottles with clean rags until we could see our faces in them. When the bottles were ready for storage in the fruit cellar I'd stay close to Grandma, hoping she'd let me help carry them for her. I loved the cellar and became excited when she'd lift the long trap door on the porch and disappear down those steep wooden steps. The tiny room below, lined with long shelves, was a magical place—cold-smelling like wet dirt, yet it was spotless. Bottles of fruit and vegetables with names and dates taped on their sealed lids stood in straight rows like tiny military men. Sacks of sugar and flour and potatoes, cans of spices and onions covered the north wall, and herbs hung from long poles in the center. The room was a miniature store underneath the house, overflowing with food. As soon as one bottle was used, two more took its place. I loved that room and enjoyed knowing it was there, even more when I grew older.

My grandmother was the most fun when she'd come home from all-day Sunday meetings. She'd be so disgruntled over my grandfather browbeating her into attending all her meetings that she'd always pick someone in the congregation as a scapegoat for her exasperation. Then, once home, she'd unmercifully mimic the poor woman she'd chosen.

"Oh, Dessie," she'd say in a squeaky voice, "those twins are just the most darling things, aren't they?" She'd raise her left hand and eyebrow in such a perfect imitation of Sister Williams that we'd choke with laughter. But Grandfather was always secretly hurt and would leave the room. Later that week, he'd be sure to quietly shovel off Sister Williams's walk, or, if it was summer, he'd mow her lawn, as if he were trying to absolve Grandma's sin for her.

Once, I asked my grandfather why we were Mormons. Why couldn't we go to a Catholic church, which seemed so much prettier with its stained glass windows and statues?

"Because you were born a Mormon under the covenant, the same as a Jew is born a Jew."

"What's a Jew?"

"A people favored by God."

"Well, then why can't *we* be Jews?"

"Because we believe that Jesus Christ is the Savior of the world."

At that it became much too complicated for me, and I left him to go sit in the middle of Grandma's flowers. There were always rows and rows of flowers circling the garden: big round fluffy peonies that we could pick apart petal by petal, and long flags the palest shades of blue and pink. We always drove to Grandma's for flowers to decorate graves on Memorial Day. Graveyards in Idaho are quiet, windy places, and the flowers would wave gaily, almost indecently, over the dead like bright laughing children.

When I was young, the names on the gravestones were faceless to me. Later we used the big, homegrown flowers to decorate Grandfather's grave, then my twin sister's grave. And it became clear to me that real people lay under the stone names. We'd leave the flowers there in the wind to dry up and die, to be thrown out later by the caretaker. One time, I tried to tell Grandma how dumb it was to dress up death. Indignant and shocked over my callousness she said, "Frank and Karon watch us paying our respects from heaven. How do you think they'd feel if we forgot about them?"

"If they're in heaven, Grandmother, I'm sure they're much too busy to care about what we're doing."

"That's not true, Missy." Then she launched into her favorite story of the day Grandfather had spoken to her from the other side of the veil. She'd been standing on a ladder trying to figure out how to put a storm window on. It wouldn't fit no matter what she did, yet she knew it was the right one for this window. Tired, frustrated, and finally crying, she started cussing Grandfather for not showing her how to put storm windows on the house before he left her alone, then she cussed him out good for dying before her, then just for dying at all. Suddenly she heard a quiet voice say, "Why don't you turn it around, Mom?" It scared her so badly she almost dropped the storm window. But finally she tried turning the window around, and it fit easily into place. This story always left me a little bit in awe, especially in my skeptical years, because I couldn't reason with it. Even though my grandmother could not boast of being a devout Mormon, she was definitely never a liar.

I remember my grandfather as a great fisherman. He knew secret holes in the Snake where fat rainbow trout grouped together facing upstream. Every year the night before fishing season opened, he'd unhook his waist-high rubber waders from a nail in the garage and check his bait box to make sure he had fresh salmon eggs and flies. His creel was a loosely woven basket with a long, leather shoulder strap that fit around his neck, and he'd line it with wet grass just before he waded into the river. I never saw him bring it back empty. Grandfather was fishing before the sun came up on the day my sister and I were born. He took my dad fishing when my little sister opened her eyes for the first time, and again when the next two babies came. My mother hated fishing.

When Grandfather fished for trout, he'd stay by one big hole for hours, circling it slowly, quietly waiting in the mountain air. He called my dad a "traveling" fisherman because he'd throw his line in a deep place only a couple of times before moving onto the next one, skipping the rapids to explore under rocky ledges. He'd walk five miles down river to every one mile Grandfather fished. I was like my father, impatient, unwilling to court the trout, giving fish one or two chances to jump at my line before I wanted to see what was around the bend. If a trout didn't bite my line quickly, he was just plain out of luck. My grandfather pointed out on more than one occasion, as I'd complain about my empty creel, that I was really the one who was out of luck.

I remember a weekend fishing trip with my grandfather soon after I turned sixteen. Troubled and restless, I hadn't wanted to go very much. I'd just had a rough experience with a young Sunday School teacher whom all the girls in my class idolized. I'd seen him, bragging, swaggering drunk, pick a fight with his friend one Saturday night, then I'd had to listen to him the next morning as he tried to teach us the Sermon on the Mount through a thick hangover. It shook me. I felt cheated in the same way I did when Mom told us there was no Santa Claus and no tooth fairy. Besides, I'd been having a lot of questions about Mormonism lately. I was irritated over its strict life-style and didn't feel I had enough freedom. Maybe I was secretly looking for a way to prove the Church wrong, because if it was a lie I was justified in leaving it behind. But if it was the truth and I left, I felt I'd be living against the way the universe had been set up. That weekend as we drove down a dusty road to reach a fork of the Snake, I talked to Grandfather about my doubts, even though I knew I was breaking his number-one rule of no-talking-while-fishing.

"The boy's faith is gone," he said about my Sunday School teacher.

"No, Grandfather, he just got back from a mission and he goes to all his meetings."

"Doesn't matter, a person's religion lies inside him. He's just a boy making a lot of mistakes. Don't you mix his mistakes up with your own religion. It's a separate thing, a private thing."

"But, Grandfather, how do you know Mormonism is the truth?"

"I just know." Clouds of dust were rolling back from the tires. We were getting close to the river now.

"But what if they're lying? How do you know they're not lying to us about the Church being true?"

He handed me my pole from the back of the truck. "Who's 'they'?"

"You know, the bishop and the elders and the Sunday School teachers—all of them." My anger sounded loud against the softly weaving pines. I had gone too far, and I dropped my head to busy myself with tying my hook. My grandfather headed down the steep trail leading to the river.

"Your faith is between you and God; others have nothing to do with it," he said over his shoulder. "You ask him about this."

I was depressed most of the morning until the sound of the river smoothed out the wrinkles in my brain. The cold water ran over moss-covered rocks—never stopping, always moving. Sun filtered through tall pines, and white birds dipped down now and then into the river upstream from my line. It was soothing and dreamlike.

After lunch we lay on some grass warm from the sun, and later I woke to see Grandfather disappearing over the ledge. Rushing to bait my hook, I was excited to try, just one time, to outfish him. At noon he'd had only two more trout than I. But evening found me three miles from camp with just two small fish flapping in my creel.

My grandfather was sitting on a rock close to the river's edge cleaning his fish when I got back. He handed me his rubber gloves and a knife as I dumped my fish next to his. I didn't like to clean fish unless I had gloves on. Though I'd never touched a snake, I thought fish must feel like snakes, slippery and slimy. So when I fished, I waited till the fish were quiet, then I'd hold them underwater to work out my hook so I couldn't feel their scales. When I cleaned them, I didn't mind slitting their white bellies open or scooping the insides out, as long as I didn't have to touch the outside of them with my bare hands. Grandfather always smiled, but he never said much about my elaborate methods. He cleaned fish quickly, easily, letting the river wash the insides of the trout white.

A woodpecker sat high in a tree across the river (I could hear him), and a few mosquitoes buzzed around my hair. Grandfather would talk soon. After the city, the mountains seemed so quiet, the silence so big and alive that you could almost touch it with your hands. The only sound was the river and the wind in the pines behind me like a thousand elves applauding the sky.

I thought of the fat trout frying in butter, so soft and flaky

you could tear the backbone out in one smooth pull. I quickly slit another fish open, already seeing its tender meat, with
brown gravy and hot powder biscuits, steaming on my plate.
Grandfather was looking far out over the river.

As he got the fire going under the heavy skillet he talked
about how weak men were, how they often failed, then tried
again to be Christian, then failed again. Yet how truth was
truth and God was God, and that never, never changed, nor
failed.

I dipped the trout in a mixture of flour and salt and listened to the woodpecker punctuating Grandfather's slow
words, digging my bare feet into the woodchips and sand,
and I really didn't understand much of what he said. But his
gravelly voice came from deep in his chest and sounded good
along with the snapping of the fire. It was good there, eating
fresh trout with my grandfather by the same Snake River that
Lewis and Clark traveled.

3

Guitars by the River

I don't know why I left home. Many of us drifted from our small Mormon towns in the sixties. Even those our age who stayed and settled into nine-to-five jobs seemed restless and troubled. No matter what our religious upbringing had been, we were still children of our times. And the beginning years of the 1960s were powerful. A great rumble of uneasiness swept the country, causing our young minds to shake with endless questioning. However, those years are so covered with clichés now that it's often difficult to look back and say what really happened. All I know is that the sixties hit us hard, shaking our most basic values. And at the same time they beckoned and promised us bright experiences on new frontiers.

Our parents were totally unprepared to cope with our confusion. They, too, were children of their times, and their advice to us was to settle down, get a job, and make some money. Maybe that broke open the first serious rift between us and them, although it had been building for years. We weren't interested in making money. Most of us had grown up looking at pictures in the daily newspaper of President Eisenhower carrying a golf bag around a lush country club, and we weren't impressed. Even then we felt materialism was a dirty word.

Our parents thought differently. I remember Mom waking us up early one morning when we were quite young. She was flushed with excitement, "There's a big surprise for you out in the car," she whispered. We ran out in our nightgowns to the blue 1955 Chevy parked in the driveway, expecting to find a kitten or at least a turtle. But we couldn't find anything, even though we looked under the seat and in the glove compartment. We walked slowly back into the house and told Mom that the surprise had been stolen.

"No," she laughed. "It's the new radio. Your dad bought a new radio for the car." She all but danced with pleasure in front of us. But Karon and I exchanged disappointed looks and shuffled back into our bedroom. It was Mother's surprise, not ours.

A new black and white television followed the radio. After that came the washer and dryer, then the golf clubs and camper-trailer. But somehow we could never get very excited —they were only things.

Of course, we had never lived through a war, or a depression either. Our parents kept reminding us of that. My dad often said, "Clean up your plate before you leave this table. I saw kids in Korea eat dandelions to keep alive. They'd kill to eat what you throw away in one meal." I'd gladly have sent my broccoli in an envelope to the Korean orphans.

Another great difference between us and our parents seemed to be our levels of curiosity. My parents were so busy scrambling out of poverty that they didn't seem to have time for asking many questions. Or maybe they had asked all their questions before we were born. Maybe they just got tired of questions. Or maybe they learned not to ask too many, flinching from noisy wars, retreating from too much knowing, trying to hold on to hope as the world crashed in bloody battles over their heads. But we were full of questions. They beat in our minds like trapped moths, causing us to ache at night with a sweet, tense pain.

I continually worried my parents with questions, and the first time I learned that my father didn't know everything, I was shattered. What I had wanted to know was so earth-shakingly important to me (though now I can't even remember what the issues were) that I felt terrified that he had no answer either. If he didn't know, then who did?

Of course, from that time on I realized there were many questions that my father had not even bothered to ask. This was unforgivable. And nothing frustrated me more than to hear my father, even jokingly, say, "Yours is not to question why, yours is but to do or die." While I was growing up he probably repeated about twice a week this couplet he'd learned in the army, until it often beat a cadence through my dreams, accompanied by the image of thousands of soldiers blindly marching like lemmings over a cliff into the sea to their deaths. I learned not to look home for fulfillment—my parents loved me, but they were too busy—and I became more hungry and thirsty as I grew older.

Some of our friends said, "Let's go to college. There they have answers." But I was afraid that college would be an extension of high school, where I'd simply learned the true definitions of four-letter words scribbled on bathroom walls.

Our Sunday School teacher said that if I was unhappy I should repent. But I wasn't sure exactly that I knew what I had done wrong. Besides, I wasn't so much unhappy as I was restless, itchy, discontented, and nervous—as if I were swaying with my horse, waiting for the gunshot to start the race and still unsure of where the racetrack lead.

We had some good teachers while I was growing up, but there were so many church meetings. And sometimes the leaders seemed busy, sitting in the chapel only with their bodies, their minds far away. I often got the feeling that our bustling MIA teacher was seeing tomorrow's dinner rather than really listening to us. On the other hand, we lived only in the moment, clutching at now. Always aware of the present, we wanted to be involved each second, engaged, absorbed into whatever was in front of us. We wanted to give ourselves to a cause, to be burned and consumed by life. Our greatest horror was to be bored.

So my attention drifted. I stopped looking to the Church for fulfillment. As soon as Mom dropped us off at MIA, we'd go through the door, into the restroom, and crawl out of the window. Others joined us, and we would sit on the banks of the river and talk to our hearts' content about whatever was important to us. Sometimes someone would bring a guitar, and we'd watch the fireflies dance across the water to John Lennon music.

We were bursting with kinetic energy, and we were hungry, wanting something but not knowing what. We just knew that whatever was churning up our insides needed to be dealt with. And the outside world beckoned like the Pied Piper. So we left town as soon as we were old enough to buy our first junk car. Many left to roam through the sixties like the Jews looking for a lost homeland.

At first our freedom was exhilarating. We learned that we could drink a beer without being struck by lightning, and we learned that no one really cared whether we swore or ate junk food or didn't take a bath for days. We were like Pinnochio in Candyland.

4

Until There's No More North

We crossed the Golden Gate Bridge for the first time at midnight. All I remember was the white line in the middle of the road. Julie was yelling, "We're here. This is it. This is really it. We made it." Cheryl was passed out in the back seat. I was intently trying to keep us from crashing through the rails into the bay.

We were stone drunk, which was sad, since we'd been thinking about crossing that bridge all day. In the morning over pancakes at Sambo's, Julie had suggested it.

"Do you realize that in my whole twenty-one years upon this polluted earth, I have never once seen the Golden Gate Bridge?" Julie was really into antipollution. In fact, Julie was into a lot of things. She jumped onto every cause she found and rode it until a louder one came along.

"Same here," I said between syrupy mouthfuls. "I've only seen it in movies."

"Sad!"

"Well, why don't we drive across the bridge while we're here. Just so we can say we've done it. We could take Cheryl to the first town past the bridge to catch her bus."

Cheryl was a friend from our high school days. Julie and I had stopped to see her in Salt Lake City, where she'd been working in a doughnut shop, and she'd asked if she could hitch a ride with us to the coast. She was getting too fat from eating so many doughnuts and wanted to go to Seattle to see a friend. We were headed for the opposite end of the coast, looking for a little sea town to spend the summer in. We didn't care where we stopped as long as there was plenty of sea and sun. Working at nickel-and-dime jobs, we'd been traveling around for the past year, drifting from town to town, killing time.

I don't know why we started drinking so early that day. I remember we went to see an old friend of Julie's who was working on a political science degree at Berkeley. He lived in one of those hill apartments that takes a key to get past the wrought-iron front gate. Inside, elegant boxes were arranged on six different levels around a swimming pool, and it smelled like mustard. Looking over the handrail on the way up to the fourth floor, I saw five Apollo-like men playing in the pool. Their swaggering insults bounced off the concrete walls like stray bullets. Next Julie's friend was offering us homemade wine that tasted like sweet soap suds. Sitting on a white sofa, under a poster of Ho Chi Minh, he quizzed Julie on the political situation in Viet Nam. I tried to choke down the wine as fast as I could, realizing we might be in for hours of "-isms" (communism, fascism, Marxism, Buddhism). But as soon as I finished the last horrid drop, Julie's greasy friend reached over and deftly refilled my glass, not missing a syllable about the poverty level in Saigon. Resigning myself to a red wine afternoon, I eased back in his wicker chair to study an old Bob Dylan poster on his wall. Someone had splashed red paint all over the face.

I can't remember if it was before or after we left the apartment that things got fuzzy. Cheryl was trying to tell me how to drive—which was funny, since the only machine she knew how to operate was a mixmaster. We were trying to find a place near the strip, a place called The Spaghetti Factory, where you could get a second plate of food free if you ate all of the first one.

In those days San Francisco's strip was fascinating. Jazz and rock and roll blared from every street corner. We walked past two small boys dancing on the sidewalk outside a nightclub. High-heeled ladies clicked along under multi-colored neon signs, and music, everywhere, seemed to beat even out of the street lights. We finally found a small door marked Spaghetti Factory that opened to a narrow spiral staircase. As we descended into smoky, spaghetti-sauce smells, we read a variety of four-letter words painted on the walls.

The inside was insane. We bumped into walls covered with old Coca-cola posters, umbrellas, chairs, fishnets, and dresses. A man with a gray beard and black coat was sitting by a wood-burning stove telling stories to two long-haired girls in Levi's. We somehow found our way to a back table and ordered wine and spaghetti. Cheryl spilled her purse all over the floor trying to find some money, and we lost Julie for twenty minutes while she tried to find the bathroom. I felt as if I was in the middle of a French film that had been cut up into little bits and pieced back together by a madman. Everything was slowed down, and snatches of conversation and the old man's story floated past my ears like pieces of seaweed in water. My head felt as if it was wrapped in cotton, and my lips as if they'd been shot with novocaine.

Unable to handle a second plate of spaghetti, we bought another bottle of wine to go and headed for a beach. Julie wanted to go swimming in the moonlight, but Cheryl was afraid of stepping on jellyfish. All I wanted was to lie down somewhere. We couldn't find a place deserted enough to take off our clothes, though Julie said she was going to anyway. But I knew she wouldn't.

Later, we were walking; we'd been walking for a long time on the wet sand, listening to the sea wash up on the beach. Julie was in front of us, weaving back and forth into the waves and out again, drinking occasionally from a bottle she had tucked under her arm. Suddenly she fell forward and lay in the sand, letting the sea wash over her. Rolling onto her side, she lifted one hand above her head and flipped the air with her fingers.

"I'm going to die right here and turn into a starfish. Go on, go on, leave me to drown. I will lie here and become part of the sea and the stars."

Cheryl was leaning on my arm, staring down at her.

"She fell down," she said in mild astonishment.

"Yep," I said. "Let's get her up; we gotta get to the bridge."

So that's how we crossed the Golden Gate Bridge: drunk, wet, and covered with sand. We missed the whole experience. Cheryl was passed out, and Julie fell asleep halfway across, in the middle of saying how exciting it was, leaving me to follow the white line.

We'd already decided somewhere between the spaghetti and the salt water that if we truly loved Cheryl, we'd take her all the way to Seattle instead of dropping her off at a bus station in her condition. So I was stuck with that white line for the rest of the night. Finally I drove myself semi-sober and pulled over to sleep in a cleared area beside the highway.

Morning light and male voices somewhere above my right ear woke me up.

"Should we knock on the window?"

"Naw, let 'em sleep. The whole crew isn't here yet. Let's wait another few minutes."

Vaguely the words drifted into my awareness. Carefully raising my head so that it wouldn't fall off my neck and roll across the floor mat, I peeked over the window rim. A crane, a bulldozer, and a couple of dump trucks were parked around our car. Three construction workers, one apparently a foreman, stood about four feet away talking together. As I watched, other cars kept pulling into the cleared area, emptying workmen into the morning. I ducked my head and whispered, "Julie, wake up!"

"Ummmmmmmmmmm."

"Julie!"

"Hey, bug off. Go back to sleep."

"Will you wake up!" I kicked her hard with my bare foot. "We're in the middle of a construction area, and I can't find the keys. Julie! I don't want to sit up until I find them. Are they underneath you?"

Julie slowly sat up, pulling parts of her body along as if they were weighted down with iron. Through half-closed eyes she looked out of her window, then slowly curled back up into a ball.

"Yup, you're right. They're tearing up all these beautiful trees to make a concrete highway."

She sounded like a Joni Mitchell song, and I seriously considered slitting her throat, but I caught a glimpse of the keys lying under the gas pedal. Apparently I'd put them above the visor last night so no one could steal the car, and they'd fallen to the sand-covered floor. Still lying on my side, I put the keys in the ignition and turned on the engine; then, taking a deep breath, I sat up quickly and gunned it. But I'd forgotten to put it in gear. Laughter exploded behind us as the car finally scrambled back onto the road.

It was then I became aware of the shape of my head. It had grown in the night to a throbbing, five-foot, red balloon. I didn't want to breathe too hard for fear it would pop and my cluttered intellectualism would spill all over the new seat covers. At the base of my mouth, blood vessels and tiny muscles were constricting with thirst. My tongue had already shriveled into a dried prune. I opened the last beer and tried to gag its lukewarm liquid past the inflamed lining of my mouth while the California sun glared off of the sea, lacerating my eyeballs. What had we done to our bodies?

Waves. Ocean. Cliffs. Seagulls. We must be headed up the coast on Highway 1. Oh, my brain was moving at an incredible speed.

It turned out to be a wine-soaked week. It was so hot that we kept drinking to handle our hangovers, which led to more hangovers.

"Let's get a motel tonight. If I don't get a bath my skin's going to crawl away to a grave." Cheryl's voice was starting to irritate me as sweat from my hands covered the steering wheel.

"One with a swimming pool. It's so hot."

"Okay, but let's get some more miles under us before we stop."

We had a goal now. We had a plan. It was Seattle—or bust. We checked into a motel with a swimming pool, but it was in Eugene, Oregon, where it was too cold to go swimming. I remember side-stepping a spider who wanted to share the shower with me. Fortunately, he drowned before either of us was seriously hurt. One good thing about Eugene was the fresh scallops and shrimp.

The next night, still in the mood for fish, we ate at a seaside bar where two old men wearing rain hats stared at us through pipe smoke. Julie, always attracted to strange men, waved and smiled as we left, drawing a cold nod from the bearded one. I was thankful that she hadn't flounced up and kissed them on the cheek.

When we got to Seattle we spent a whole day lying on the grass by a fountain in the World's Fair park, watching the Space Needle elevator go up and down, up and down, taking one load of people after another up to eat in a restaurant whose only claim to fame was that it was closer to the clouds than the McDonald's on the corner. Julie was fascinated by that Space Needle. She loved anything that was above ground: birds, planes, missiles, moons.

Then Cheryl decided she didn't want to stay in Seattle. She called her friend and he'd left for Alaska the week before. Some people just keep heading north until there's no more north, but not us. We wanted to go south in the worst way. I was sick of salmon and oysters, rock beaches and rain. Besides, the sun was in the south. It lived and ate and slept there. Julie was quiet through Oregon and northern California, Cheryl just kept eating, and I took pictures of redwoods and ferns and huge yellow butterflies.

Our bodies grew used to the movement of the car, but when we reached Big Sur we knew we had to stop. I thought we'd entered heaven. We rented a house on a clamming beach in the first little town we came to after the cliffs, and I went to work as a motel maid to support us. (It was my turn.) Cheryl roamed the beaches looking for dead lobsters, and Julie studied Zen Buddhism at the local library.

All three of us kept drinking. It numbed us, helped us put off thinking about what we were doing. And it pushed away the future, which we were no longer so eager to jump into. There were times when I was sure the skies were raining wine. We partied until the whole universe seemed to throb with a dull headache.

One hung-over morning, we were sitting on the sand waiting for our tongues to resurrect. I was sucking an orange, watching endless breakers roll in. An old fishing boat was anchored about half a mile out, and seagulls played around its mast. I loved those seagulls. They flew and lit and flew again in lyrical patterns above the blue-green sea. Cheryl was almost asleep. The sea could do that to you. Julie was sick; as usual she had grossly overdone it the night before. There was never anything halfway about Julie.

"You know what?" she said to the seagulls. "This is stupid."

I tossed an orange peeling into the waves.

"I mean it." She turned towards me. "What are we doing?"

"What do ya want to do?"

"I don't know. I want something, but not this, not anymore."

I kept peeling my orange, although I'd sucked all of the juice out of it through a small hole. "A guy told me last night that the trains slow way down when they go through San Luis," I told her. "He said it's easy to jump one and ride it to Monterey."

"That's stupid." Julie wasn't angry; the words sounded flat, like a pie tin dropping on a sidewalk.

"Well," I tried again, "another guy told me that if we wanted to go to Hawaii, he knows of a steamer that might give us passage if we hire on as assistant cooks. Do you want to do that?"

"So what's in Hawaii? Nothing! Just like here."

I kept sucking on my orange even though it tasted dry and stringy. The fishing boat was moving now and the gulls were screaming. Julie stood up and watched the waves for a while.

"See ya," she said. Then she started walking away. I followed her with my eyes until she was nothing but a tiny dot on the sand. Cheryl wiggled up beside me, blurry-eyed and cross, and I told her I would probably be going home to Idaho in a couple days. I missed my little brother. He was two years older now, and I wondered if he'd remember me pulling him onto the front of my saddle for a horseback ride.

5

The Trip Up

But I didn't go home. I hitchhiked south to Los Angeles to see my twin sister, leaving the balmy air of Big Sur with little regret. Nothing made much sense these days. There was no center or clear base. The days were fuzzy. I worried about my eyes, sure that I needed glasses because my vision seemed blurred. I promised myself to make an appointment for an eye check-up as soon as I got to Los Angeles. I felt as if I were in a huge movie theater and someone was turning the dimmer switch on the lighting. So I spent the days trying not to think. Life became an avoidance game.

Karon was working at T.R.W. making diodes for missiles. "It's not as fancy as it sounds," she said. "I work with a lettering machine in a factory."

I camped out in a lawn chair at her apartment swimming pool for a couple weeks until my money ran out, then got a job at the same concrete factory. We ate honey sandwiches at lunch around a plastic table and snorted Methedrine in the bathroom on our breaks. Karon was into white witchcraft, and I'd often stumble over strange bodies sprawled on her living room floor in varying degrees of trance-like states. They swore they were reaching for the cosmos, but I was sure they came over for free drugs and music.

Los Angeles was a strange place towards the end of the sixties: fast, turbulent, wild—a snakepit of different trips. Everyone was some sort of fanatic; everyone had a cause. And though there was still a lot of hype in the wind about brotherhood, peace, and love, no one trusted anyone. Health nuts disliked Jesus people. Speed freaks hated junkies. People who took acid disdained people who were hooked on downers. And, of course, straights, wearing suits and ties, didn't fit anywhere. Intellectuals flitted around the edges of the drug scene, with their loose, Indian-made muslin shirts and wire-rimmed glasses, but they were careful not to swallow anything that might send them down the hole with Alice to Wonderland. They bought enough grass to smoke over their late night Jasmine tea, and kept it in a plastic baggie taped to the underside of a toilet seat so that it could be flushed quickly in case the boogeyman came.

Then there were those who sincerely wanted to break through the borders of their own reality. They felt there was something beyond what they had. And though they'd thrown out all their traditional values, their quest was a religious one. Their favorite drugs were L.S.D., mescaline, and peyote. They felt that if they could crash all the lines of demarcation in their minds, all the strict rules of reality that bound them and held them, they would see God. And they were intensely interested in knowing what he looked like. Some believed that the state of "beyondness" they were searching for would resemble the Eastern concept of Nirvana; some felt it would look like the end of *2001: A Space Odyssey* —we would be stripped of everything except innocent child-likeness and float endlessly through the multi-colored cosmos. Some felt we would see Buddha or Christ or find out that we, ourselves, were God. Some felt that once past the boundaries of our own minds, we'd regress beyond birth and embrace Eugene O'Neill's ape. Others felt that the whole inner workings of the universe were made up of high forms of intense energy.

But the one common element that they were all sure they would find was love: a love so incredibly bright that it would burn away impurities and melt everyone together in ecstatic giving and giving and giving. I was drawn to this group, and began to spend hours in apartments filled with plants and bamboo chairs and imported incense, spreading peanut butter on foul-tasting peyote buttons to choke them past my taste buds, and listening to theory after complicated theory zip past my head.

Fired by the discussions of different utopias, I bought books by Huxley, Hesse, and Thoreau, and, of course, Alan Watts, who was on the fringes of Timothy Leary's group. I read about Leary's experiments with L.S.D. at Harvard and followed his current career avidly. I spent hours studying Zen, intrigued by its strict discipline. Perhaps I was drawn by the concept of gaining complete control over one's body because I knew we were slowly losing power over our own bodies through our heavy use of drugs.

And finally, after nearly a hundred L.S.D. trips of my own, it slowly dawned on me that I was no longer in control of my life. However, at the same time, I was experiencing mind-boggling freedom—from language, and from my own inhibitions and self-consciousness, as if I were rising above "me," even above the concept of "me-ness." I seemed to be breaking apart my normal modes of perception, and much of what I saw and felt was indescribable. And yet, did I see God? No. Ultimately, I saw each of us reaching unscalable plateaus of isolation, as if we stood still on blocks of barren ice, floating above and around each other, but never connecting or touching, and I became terrified. The trip up was too quick and artificial. And I always had to come down again. Yet each time the drug's influence left my body, the world was a little more distorted.

Suddenly, now, instead of breaking through my own reality, I wanted things back the way they were. I wanted the safe boundaries again. We had gone too far. We had tried to reach heaven by swallowing a pill, and we had profaned sacred ground.

I was quickly losing my ability to function in daily situations. I had trouble in talking. Sometimes when I spoke, Karon's face told me that what I'd said did not relate at all to what was happening around me. My sense of time became distorted, and I would gather up my lunch sack and coat at work barely two hours after I'd arrived there, sure that it must be five o'clock already. Or I'd jump out of the bathtub in a panic, thinking I had soaked for hours past the time I was supposed to be at work, only to find that barely ten minutes had ticked off the clock. Going to the grocery store became a nightmare. There were too many lights, too much noise, too many women with crying kids and headaches, who seemed to reach out and drop their pain in my shopping cart as they passed until I could barely push it along the aisles.

Choosing between chicken soup and tomato soup was impossible. I was hungry all the time, but to get at mandarin oranges wrapped in bright paper and tin seemed beyond my capabilities—too much work and too much trouble. I suddenly became afraid of food poisoning, though we were polluting our bodies daily with poisonous drugs, and finally I would buy only bean sprouts and fresh fruits to eat.

One morning I woke up about four and heard Karon crying in her room across the hall. They were hard sobs—hopeless, uncontrollable, choking. I lay still for hours listening to her, unable to move or think or feel, tracing the plaster pattern on the ceiling over and over again.

Then on January 30, 1969, the Tet offensive began, barely three weeks after we'd heard a speech by General Westmoreland promising us that the Viet Cong would soon surrender. They'd had it, we had been told; ''Charlie's all pooped out.'' The next thing we saw on the news was the United States ambassador to Saigon firing a pistol out of the window of the United States embassy at an advancing Red army. At first I was sure it was just another late-night John Wayne movie. Then

Martin Luther King and Bobby Kennedy were killed, assassinated by freaks—people who no longer lived within the boundaries of reality. And I clawed the walls in panic. The world—the reality—I wanted so desperately to get back to seemed to be churning and turning upside down like some obscene carnival ride. My brain felt as if it would split open like a rotted watermelon, and I'd sit by the pool for hours, studying the water moving.

Then one night I found myself on a bus headed for Idaho. I don't remember even saying good-bye to Karon. All I knew was that it felt good to be passing through darkened towns and deserts, rolling towards a part of the land I knew.

I longed for something I was sure of, some proof that the world was not all bad. When I got home maybe I'd load up a horse and a sleeping bag and drive to the mountains for a couple of days to ride through the aspen trees; or maybe I'd just sit in a lawn chair under the weeping willow in our backyard and watch the dogs play. Maybe I'd visit my grandfather's windy grave and lie in the tall grass to sleep for a whole sunny afternoon. Idaho sounded good; and as I leaned back in the darkened bus, I felt relief moving through the vast tiredness of my body and mind. My family loved me.

I knew Mom's homemade bread and Sunday roast would still smell the same. And Dad's horses would still stamp and snort in the early morning cold. And mice would still run out of the haystack every time I pulled down a fresh bale of hay.

6

And Again, Unto Dust

She looked bad. I didn't think she was going to make it. Somehow I knew she'd gone too far.

She started home from Los Angeles, and her car broke down in Tonopah, Nevada. She called me, collect, and I drove down through the sagebrush and the heat to get her.

I found her sitting—too quietly—on a vinyl couch next to some slot machines, her hands folded over the purse on her lap, a small suitcase at her feet. She looked burnt, out of step. Her eyes were red and slightly swollen. Even so, she sat primly, just as she'd sat on a high school stage four years ago, wearing a blue formal to run for Miss Bonneville.

"Hey, how's it going?" I spoke as softly as I could over the clash of the slot machines. She turned her head, but her eyes had trouble in finding my face.

"Oh, you're here," she said almost in surprise. I picked up her suitcase and headed for the car.

"Where'd you sleep last night?"

"I just sat on the couch. The doorkeeper bought me a coke." She quickly wiped tears away. I could tell it had been a long wait for her, a long night. She had always waited for me, and I had always been late.

Karon was milder than I, more shy, more careful. I was the tomboy, the talker, the charmer. Self-centered and aggressive, I stole every show, simply by my energy, while Karon looked on from the sidelines. Walking in the shadows must have been almost unbearable for her at times. For me, though, Karon was my identity—my mirror. Who was I? I was part of a set. I was so important that Those-in-Charge-of-the-Universe had made two of me.

I remember the first time Karon had refused to dress alike. It was the summer family reunion when we were twelve. She'd sat on the bed with her arms folded while Mom coaxed, then bribed, then threatened. Karon just shook her head slowly. "No, I want my own clothes." I couldn't understand what the fuss was all about. Whether we dressed alike or not, we'd still get to play with our cousins and eat ice cream and watermelon. But Karon stood firm against all Mom's threats.

Now, as we walked outside to the car, the heat was intense, burning through the top of my head. Dust rose up around our shoes and shimmered in the thick air. *Why would anyone want to live in Nevada,* I thought to myself.

"Are you hungry? Want some breakfast?" I motioned towards a truck stop across the street. She looked around at the old wood buildings and shrugged.

"I just want to go home."

"Okay. Why don't you lie down in the back seat? Bet you're tired." I still couldn't figure out what she'd been swallowing. She moved slowly, almost as if she was drunk, yet there was a rigidity about her that suggested amphetamines.

"No, I'm fine, I'm fine. Let's go."

As she leaned over to roll down the back window, her purse fell off her lap and spilled all over the floor mat. There, lying among eyeshadow and small change, was the biggest bottle of reds I'd ever seen. Phenobarbitol: a four-star downer. Some packets of Methedrine also fell under the seat. We both scrambled for the drugs quickly, shoving them under the floor mats and pillow. All we needed was to get busted in this dustbowl of a town. As I sat up to see if anyone was walking near the car, I automatically glanced at Karon's arms. No needle marks, at least. She must be on a speedball: snorting speed in the morning to get through the day, then dropping downers to handle the speed. A bad trip. To break the cycle and get back to your own rhythms was almost impossible. Most of the people I knew who had been caught up on speedballs had had to dry out at an institution, and Karon had never been big on institutions.

"Whew," I whistled. "Do you think you have enough reds?"

"It's too hard to get them in Idaho," she said defensively, handing me some crosstops for the drive home.

As we drove across the desert, Karon sat perfectly still, not even blinking. A couple times, I thought she must have fallen asleep, but glancing in the rearview mirror I'd see her eyes wide, staring down at her purse, her face set like a skull. Yet there was an uncomfortable looseness about her, as if her bones were almost on the verge of falling away from each other. I got the feeling that if she opened her mouth, her jaw would disconnect and fall into her lap.

After we stopped in a small town in Idaho for gas, she started talking, ripping along in the rise and fall of a speed jag. One sentence—one word in a sentence—would lead her onto something else. She'd start describing the sailboat Dan had bought, then move on to the health value of eating seaweed. She talked until she kept getting into corners, and I could tell she was even scaring herself. Then the catatonic looseness started again. I wondered how she was swallowing those pills dry. We didn't have any water.

The drive seemed long. The sand and sagebrush rippled in the heat. Dust rolled across the hills to the left, and my forehead and neck felt too tight. I'd looked forward so much to seeing Karon, talking to her, just being with her. I needed her. But I was carrying home an empty shell: bones wrapped up in skin. Even though she had clear moments, she was really

wacko. I knew there was not much chance of cutting through
the cobwebs in her head. Besides, what did I know? I was
trying to claw my own way out of a hole I'd dug with drugs.
Karon, though, had fallen all the way through the bottom.
She wasn't there for me, and if she was gone, we could all go.
On the radio Glen Campbell sang, "Where's the playground,
Susie? You're the one who's supposed to know your way
around."

"You'd better turn your lights on," Karon said from the
backseat. Glancing around I realized that the sun had set.
There was barely enough light to see the white line.

"Thanks."

"You okay? I can't drive, ya know."

"I know. I'm fine. I'm okay. I think I'll just pull over for a
minute."

We both got out and leaned against the warm car. The
desert was silent, and I eased into its atmosphere. After Led
Zepplin tapes and the sound of the engine, it felt good. My
ears rang with the quiet as I slipped off my sandals to feel the
warm sand. There were a million stars already, close up, like a
huge, painted postcard.

"You still into astrology?" Karon asked.

"Naw, I've been reading a lot about religion."

"What religion?"

"Oh, Eastern mostly, Zen and stuff. Catholicism. I kinda
like all that ceremony."

"Mormonism?"

"I don't like Mormons." I turned my head away from her.
She'd hit a sore spot.

"Aw, c'mon. You just met a lot of bad ones." She glanced
off across the desert. "I liked Primary," she said. "Remember
Sister Hart?"

I nodded, smiling at the ground. "Who could forget her?"
Hart had been the terror of our Sunday School and Primary
days. I remembered one Primary afternoon after opening
exercises when she'd grabbed Karon's arms.

"You think it's real cute to giggle in the chapel, don't you, young lady. Well, we'll see how cute you think it is to go without a treat later." She'd leaned down close to Karon's face and gritted her teeth. "In-the-chapel-we-sit-quietly-and-think-about-Jesus-do-you-understand?" Then she'd marched down the hall to set out pictures in the classroom. Shaking, Karon turned around and headed for the door.

"Wait," I whispered. "If you leave, you'll get it worse." Carolyn grabbed her other arm and we walked her to class. When Sister Hart handed out the sugar cookies, she made a big deal out of passing up Karon. So when the cookies got to us, we just shook our heads no, too timid to say it out loud, but trying to help Karon as much as we could. Now, thinking about Sister Hart made me laugh. She must have been an awfully unhappy woman.

"I started reading the New Testament in Los Angeles, and I feel like I've finally found God," Karon said quietly.

"Oh? Where is he?"

"Well, I guess I'm not sure. But I want . . ."

"Now which god are you talking about?"

"The one we learned about in Primary. It's me, though, it's me that's all wrong . . ."

She sounded so foggy. And she was wearing sort of a sick smile as she said, "But I do know where we're going after this life."

"Oh, yeah? Well, I'm getting cold. You bring a sweater?"

"No. Now listen, really, the problem is that it's all tied up with loving people, and in order to live, you have to relate. And I'm so far away from people. I can't seem to . . . They seem so far away." She looked puzzled, then shivered. "I guess I just want to go home."

I helped her back into the car. She'd seemed clear and in control when we'd stopped, but now she was like a jellyfish. She mumbled to herself for the next hour as I flipped channels on the radio, trying to figure out how to sneak her past our parents. It was a long drive.

Karon rented a house the next day in town, and her boxes
arrived on the bus. I helped her deposit them on the kitchen
floor, but several days later all she had unpacked was her
coffee pot and some cups. Mom would keep asking her if she
needed help moving in, and Karon would say no, she was just
fine; then she'd go home and unpack a poster of Bob Dylan
or some towels and blankets that night. But she'd lose interest
fast, and the boxes just sat unopened on her floor.

She came to Mom's for dinner on Sunday. A big affair. The
whole family was there. I walked in from riding Dad's horse
to find her sprawled on the couch picking at Scott's guitar.

"Want me to show you a chord I learned?" I asked.

"No, I don't want you to show me anything," she
snapped. She was coming down hard. Mom was rattling pans
in the kitchen, happy about the smells of roast beef and sweet
potatoes and homemade bread. Karon jumped up and started
pacing.

"I gotta go, I gotta go!"

"Sit down," I whispered. "Mellow out a little. Mom's
been cooking all day for this dinner."

She looked at me out of the corner of her eyes and her
voice turned velvety and sarcastic. "Well, sure, sister dear,
anything you say."

This wasn't Karon. During dinner it got worse. I could tell
she didn't have much saliva left to mix with her food. Speed:
lots of it, I thought. She tried, she really made a supreme
effort, to tap into what was going on, but it was no use; she
was too jagged, and she was walking way outside the reality
of the dinner table. She finally just gave in to the storm raging
inside of her, and when someone asked her what her plans
were now that she was home, she flipped. Shoving her chair
back, she shouted, "I don't care, I don't care, I gotta go
home."

Everyone stopped eating and stared. I flinched. No one
moved. There was no sound. I raised my hand up to shade
my eyes to block out her craziness, as if it might dissolve

while I wasn't looking and drain away until only Karon was left sitting at the table. Karon dropped her head, then raised it to look out of the window. She then pulled her chair back and calmly tried to cut up her meat as if she were at a royal tea party, as if she hadn't just spilled her craziness all over Sunday dinner.

Later, while driving her home, I said disgustedly, "You're not relating at all; you're not even coming close."

"I know, I know," she said quietly.

I thought I was the only one who could reach in and pull her out of her cobwebs, but I felt helpless.

It was hot on the day that Mom told my little sister to take the lawn mower to town and mow Karon's lawn. I was supposed to drive her in, and I remember hollering at Becky to hurry as I loaded the mower in the trunk. Hung over from the night before, I felt nauseated from the heat. Besides, the absurdity of Mom wanting Karon's lawn mowed when Karon hadn't even unpacked her clothes irritated me.

I hadn't seen Karon for a couple of days, but I knew she was worse. Cheryl and Linda had been worried about her the previous evening when they caught up with me at the local bar. "She was acting so strange. You'd better go talk to her."

"I'll drive by on my way home."

"We asked her if she wanted a ride home because she said she wanted to go home, and she just stared and said no. 'No, I just want to go home,' she said, just like that, and we said, 'Yeah? Well, do you want a ride?' She just waved her hand and said she wanted to walk by the river for a while, so we said, 'We'll come with you,' and she said, 'No, no, you can't. You have to stay here.'"

"So is she just out there in the dark walking home?"

"Well, no, this was about nine. Hey, where have you been anyway? We've been looking for you for a couple hours."

"I'll go over there. I'll go talk to her." But I never made it. Things got crazier and crazier, and by the time I got home, it was 4:00 A.M.

Now I had to sweat in this hot car while my little sister found her sandals. Just as soon as I dropped her off I was going to crawl back in bed.

When we finally pulled into Karon's driveway, I noticed her porch light was still on. Curtains waved at us from an open bedroom window. The long grass did make the place look shabby. After I unloaded the lawn mower, I almost went in to talk to Karon, but my head was pounding too loudly and the sun was too hot.

"Tell Karon I'll be in later and bring her some bagels. Call me when you're done." As I pulled away I saw little Becky in the rearview mirror, standing by the lawn mower and looking up at Karon's windows. "I should go back and help her," I thought. "She's too small to handle that jungle by herself." But I was too strung out to turn around.

Becky found her lying on the bedroom carpet. The blood in her face had drained to one side, turning it blue. Becky backed slowly out of the room, then ran three blocks to a friend's.

"She's dead," her friend told her when they got back to the house. "You'd better call your sister."

"Now, slow down," I said, gripping the phone tighter. "I can't understand what you're saying."

"I said she won't move," Becky said quietly into the phone. I could tell she must be at a neighbor's house, using their phone. "I can't get her up; she won't get up." Becky's voice started to catch in her throat.

"All right, calm down. Wait on the porch for me. I'm coming right in." As I peeled out of the driveway, I remember, I cussed Karon's stupidity. I knew she must have overdosed on those stupid reds, and I kept trying to figure out how I was going to get her stomach pumped without Mom and Dad and the stupid cops finding out. How were we going to lift her into the car? What doctor should I call? Our family doctor was definitely out. Maybe the emergency room was the best idea; besides, it was the closest.

The first thing I saw as I turned down her street was the cop car. I hit the steering wheel hard with my hand. The neighbor, of course, the neighbor whose house Becky phoned from must have called them. Now Karon had really done it up big. How was I ever going to get her out of this one? She'd probably get busted good for those reds. The cops still thought this was a relatively drug-free town. Part of me wanted to keep right on driving.

The next thing I remember was Becky running towards me, crying and shaking all over. She was a mess.

"They say she's dead; you don't think she is, do you? I just talked to her yesterday. Go do something. Go in there and do something." She hung on my arm as I kept walking towards the door.

"Shhh now, who's in there? Did you call Dad?"

"No, no, do we have to? He'll have a fit, I mean a real fit."

I noticed the neighbor standing off to the side of the porch with his hands in his pockets. Becky's friend and a little boy on a Big Wheels were on the sidewalk. I could hear the police car radio flipping off and on in the background as I walked through the door. My only thought was to get those cops off Karon so she wouldn't be confused and scared by them.

I knew she wasn't responsible; she was like a sick, hurt animal, but they didn't know that, and cops were weird. They were the enemy. Two of them walked out of her bedroom.

"Are you the sister?"

"None of your business," I said, trying to get past them. The younger one held me back.

"You'd better not go in there. You can't do anything to help her. She's been dead for quite a while."

"How do you know? Are you sure?" He looked down at the floor, and I suddenly saw that he was shaking also.

"We're sure. You'd better go next door and call your parents." I didn't start shaking until I dialed the number of my dad's office.

I'd never seen my father cry. He didn't cry right away. After the cops took him in the bedroom, he paced quickly back and forth in the front room, like an animal, rubbing his

forehead. Then he swore. Then he turned to me and Becky
and said, "See? See what drugs do?" Then he paced back and
forth again. I remember thinking how absurd that sounded.

"Go call your mother at work. Don't tell her anything,
just say for her to meet us downstairs."

We drove to get Mom in Dad's company car. I hadn't
been inside it for years. It smelled like leather and saddle
soap. Mom was waiting for us, and I could tell she knew
something awful had happened. She got in the car, and we
pulled to the next stoplight before anyone said anything.

"What's the matter, Don? What's happened?"

That's when Dad cried. I could tell he wasn't used to
crying because he broke into great gulping sobs, and I
thought he was going to choke or have a heart attack. He just
couldn't get the words out. In the meantime the light
changed, and someone behind us honked his horn.

"Do you want me to drive, Dad?" I whispered from the
back seat.

"No," he snapped. "I don't want you to ever drive my
car. I can drive. I can drive." My dad always got mad when he
was scared.

The relatives and Relief Society sisters came in herds that
afternoon bringing pies and cakes and casseroles until there
was no place left to put food. Whenever someone new rang
the doorbell, Mom jumped up to get them a plate and napkin,
no forks or cups, just plates and napkins, sometimes just napkins, before she fell back onto the couch as if she'd just forgotten what she was doing. Dad just sat in his chair with his
arms folded. I eased out of the back door later and drove back
to Karon's. Two of my aunts were already there, loading her
boxes into a car. They hugged me and told me to go home
and eat. I wished they'd leave so I could be alone with
Karon's things for a while.

It was a big funeral. Lots of family. My parents were heart-
broken and ashamed. The speakers all very carefully and suc-
cessfully sidestepped the suicide thing, but it blared out loudly from the coffin, fingering almost everyone there.

At the cemetery long-haired Max, who had tried so many times to talk Karon straight ("You don't need drugs to find truth," he'd say over and over, until Karon would avoid him as much as possible), climbed out of an old station wagon, and my mother freaked. "Oh, Don, there's one of them now. Oh, no, he's coming over here."

Max stood across the casket from me staring at the flowers, his face expressionless, his hands in his pockets, stepping back to let my uncles pass. He and I stayed longer than anyone else at the cemetery, until the men stood ready to lower the coffin, and longer. Not for sentimental reasons, but because we didn't know what else to do, where else to go. We watched for a while the mound of dirt they'd thrown on top of Karon, then wandered around the cemetery looking at other graves until the sun went down.

7

John Hole's Bridge

Margo and I stumbled to a front table close to the stage. The band nodded in our direction, and David, the lead guitar player, signaled the waitress for us. I remember the music pounding so loudly that it moved the table under our drinks in the old, high-ceilinged bar, which was drafty even in the summer and always smelled like pretzels. The tables surrounded a wooden dance floor, and multi-colored strobe lights flicked on and off from the band's platform, hiding from us the dirty spots on our glasses, making people glow with moving dots of color. We were earlier than the usual bar crowd, but most everyone we knew ended up here before the night was over.

Sucking lemons and salt we washed down straight shots of tequila to make the time pass faster, and the night slowly became more distorted as the electric organ throbbed out blues and rock. The band was good. No one danced. Everyone just sat and drank and watched them play. David, his hair still short from Viet Nam, quickly took over the lead with his guitar when the organ player lost it. He was good at cover-up

work. The bartender, also owner, never guessed that most of
the band played while shot up on speed every night. Or
maybe he did know, but just didn't care as long as they drew
the kids in.

David didn't take drugs anymore. Living by the Snake
River with a big Alaskan husky, he drank beer all day on his
dock, switching to Tom Collins at night. He held a history
degree from USC and was an excellent musician. Sometimes
after the bar closed, we'd fall asleep on his floor while he
played Bob Dylan songs to us. David hated drugs now and
lectured us all the time, especially me.

"You're stronger than the rest," he'd say to me. "You
gotta get out before you get sucked under. Margo'll follow
you, but she's not going to make it unless you help her."
David and his brilliant friends were remnants from the old
Haight Ashbury district, and I loved to hear him tell stories
about the beginning of the hippie movement there. He said it
was good then; there were still some high ideals and good
people flashing around. But things got messy quick in Haight
Ashbury, especially for David's friends. They were burned
one night by a speed-freak dealer who sold them bad stuff.
And by morning two of them were dead, one was lying in an
intensive care unit, and two more were walking up the middle of a freeway off-ramp.

"My best friend and I were trying to walk home to
Idaho." David would pause dramatically. "Only he never got
here. He's in a mental ward in Fresno with mush in his head.
They have to move his body for him every hour because he
can't move or talk or think. I limped back to Idaho, practical-
ly carrying my head under my arm to keep it from splattering
all over the highway, just in time for Uncle Sam to shove me
on a plane for Nam."

I'd quickly try to change the subject before he got into
war stories, because once David got moving, he'd really blow
steam. Pacing up and down in front of his rock fireplace, he'd
describe the gore and the horror, waving his hand in the air
like a band conductor, his voice shrieking at the rafters.

Sometimes I only believed half of what he said, but I loved to watch him get excited, because no one cared that much about anything anymore. It got boring fast though. Everyone knew drugs were bad, and no one cared. Drugs were still the forbidden fruit, Peter Pan's gang. They blurred the edges of our isolation and glued us together into oblivious groups. But David hated drugs.

Suddenly he stepped off the stage, carrying his microphone with him, and sat down at our table. Looking at him lounging in the chair next to me, I wondered again what it'd be like to fall in love with him. Probably a lot of trouble. Everything was trouble lately. Five or six people craned their necks towards us to see what he was doing. I wondered, too. He leaned over, brushed the hair out of my eyes, and started to sing me a love song. Nice gesture, but I was too stoned to care. He sang into the microphone softly, looking right at me, and a huge high school giggle rose up the back of my throat. I bit down hard and shook the hair back into my eyes. He was too serious, too sweet. Besides, it didn't hurt me to let him make a fool out of himself. David hated drugs and was getting to be a real pain about it lately.

But there were many who were quitting the drug scene. I couldn't help but wonder what they were going back to. Where did you go from where we had been? My friend Nick quit cold one late afternoon in the spring. He flushed all his pills, and left for the mountains to live for a summer with Indians, where he learned how to make sheepskin coats. He got so good and made so many that he went to Los Angeles to sell them. I talked to him just before he went, and he swore he'd cleaned his body out for good. "I don't even smoke anymore," he said.

But peddling his coats in a restaurant on the strip, he overheard Christy Reed, a singer-songwriter, worrying about money. She was trying to figure out how to furnish a room in her twelve-room house. Nick laughed out loud in the next booth. They were married a year later and bought a ranch near Spokane, where they rode horses all summer. She bought him a new red car and expensive drums, even taught him to play backup in her band. Before the next spring, while she was touring in Australia, Nick overdosed in her marble bathroom in Los Angeles. Christy Reed sent a tape to be played at his funeral in which she raged against the evils of drugs. It was a boring tape. We knew drugs were evil. Nick's sickness went deeper than that, and we ached over his death because it was our death, too.

Things got so crazy. There were more and more suicides. Junk drugs, cut with strychnine, showed up everywhere, and there were more and more bad trips.

Some mornings I'd wake up with a semi-clear head in my two-room apartment with patchwork carpeting. I'd study the plants on the window shelf that kept dying from marijuana smoke and wonder what I was doing. It was like raising my head above water for a moment and seeing for the first time how muddy the river had grown. *This is where it all stops,* I'd think, and I'd swear I was going to quit crucifying myself. Then Crazy Mary would show up with some new crosstops, and talk me into driving to Yellowstone Park with her, and the day would be good as we drove through pines. I'd feel something tugging at me, as if somewhere deep within me some great, bright truth was about to be uncovered. My muscles would strain hard after it. And I'd drop more and more speed, feeling like I wasn't high enough yet to reach it.

Over and over the same thing happened. We'd have so many bad trips that it'd finally dawn on our numb minds to quit. But just as we'd swear we were quitting, we'd have one good trip to end all trips, so good it'd keep us hanging in there for what promised to be an explosive discovery of the universe. But nothing ever exploded except our own minds.

One late afternoon I was sitting on the kitchen table looking out of the window at the sun patterns on the back porch, considering the flatness of my life and of the lives of my friends. We were not filled with burning passions any-more, nor did we crusade any longer for our hundred heartfelt causes. There was no laughter, nor even much crying now. And I knew it wasn't just me; I heard it in the voices and the silences of my friends, like the sound of a heart monitor after the patient dies on the operating table. Looking into the mirror on the opposite wall, I thought again how much my face had aged—hollow, tight-skinned with shadows, hungry.

The sound of someone knocking drifted through the cotton that seemed to wrap my mind, and I pushed the cat away from my leg in irritation. I couldn't think of anyone I wanted to see and several I didn't want to see. But the knocking insisted, and I finally opened the door to find two very clean boys dressed in dark suits. Knowing I couldn't relate to anyone in suits, no matter what they were selling, I mumbled, "I don't have any money," and began to close the door. It never occurred to me that they might be missionaries. This was Mormon country; why would they send Mormon missionaries to Mormons?

"No," the shorter one giggled, "we're not salesmen. We're from The Church of Jesus Christ of Latter-day Saints, and we've got an important message for you. May we come in and talk to you about our Church?" He rattled the last part off like he'd rehearsed it in his sleep.

At the same time I became aware that the taller boy was looking at me intently. As I glanced resentfully towards him, I saw his face soften. He seemed to see straight into my heart, then he said very gently, "Won't you please let us talk to you. We felt so strongly that we should stop here. I know that what we have to say will help you."

For a few moments I froze, then feeling shame over the tears starting up behind my eyes—it had been so long since someone had spoken with such kindness to me—I started to close the door. "No," I whispered, unable to look at him any longer. "No, thank you. Not now."

Leaning heavily against the wall, I listened to them talk in low voices for a moment, then I heard them slowly walk away. Suddenly I felt furious. I should have told them what I thought of organized religion. I couldn't care less about which church was true. I didn't even know if there was a God or not. Who did they think they were, anyway? The cat brushed up against my arm, purring for some attention, and I knocked her roughly off the back of the table.

Now David brought me back suddenly to the bar by playing my favorite Beatles song, "While My Guitar Gently Weeps." His fingers moved lightly, smoothly, over the strings, and he and the band and the people in the bar and the whole town and universe seemed joined together in one giant, quiet sob. The chords fell like tears into the audience.

Margo's chin fell off her hand again. Her hair covered her face so I couldn't see her eyes. What'd she take tonight? I couldn't remember. Earlier I'd watched her closely to see that she didn't overdo it again, but somewhere in the last hour I'd lost track of her beside me. Sitting up in my chair, I moved her purse over. Margo ate anything now. Slightly swaying with David's music, she didn't even know I was there.

Margo was a friend of Karon's first. Then, a couple of years ago, we all moved into a basement apartment across from a big Catholic church, and the three of us became inseparable. She was pretty, and there was a quietness about her that made her easy to be with. She came from a big, very poor family, and she always held a job longer than the rest of us. Usually she wore a headband, but it never kept her long black hair out of her eyes, and she made me laugh. Sometimes all I had to do was look at her to start laughing. I envied her and how she was amused by such small things. She loved the first snowfall, and if she was working, she'd always take that night off and insist we drive as far as we could into the mountains where it was snowing the hardest. As soon as the car stopped, she'd jump out to roll in the fields and make snow angels in the moonlight. We'd put Isaac Hayes on the tape deck, and turn it loud and play in the snow with our dogs until our eyelashes were crusted with ice.

Or sometimes Margo would just sit on our musty couch, listening to the Moody Blues, watching rain dripping down our windows for hours. Or she'd pour apple syrup and peach jam over vanilla ice cream and hold each spoonful in her mouth until it dissolved. When she learned how to make candles out of paraffin wax and color crayons, she was ecstatic; in the next month she made enough candles to cover one wall of our apartment.

Once, we found her sitting all alone on a front pew in the Catholic church across the street. She said she was just watching the candles. One had flickered and gone out, and Margo had quietly slipped up and tried to light it again from another candle. But hearing someone open a side door, she quickly sat down again without getting it lit.

Margo had dropped in on Karon in Los Angeles right after I'd left for Idaho. Then she'd stayed in Hermosa Beach after Karon left for home, long enough to get hooked on junk. She'd been busted for carrying drug paraphernalia, and after two weeks in the L.A. jail for women, she had called her half-sister in Idaho for a ride home. Her sister had called me to go along for the ride. Getting busted was probably the luckiest thing that'd ever happened to Margo. She was going under for the last time when they took her to jail.

We finally found her in a dive in Venice, living with the bass player of a local band. She was wrecked. Sleeping on a torn mattress covered with cracker crumbs and candy wrappers, she looked like a scarecrow someone had tossed into the dumpster.

"Let's go, Margo. Where's your stereo?" I could tell her sister was disgusted.

"I dunno . . ." She was trying hard to think. "We had a party and this guy walked out with it."

"Didn't you try to stop him?"

"Naw."

"Get your things."

"Where we going?"

"You called us to come and get you, remember?" Her sister's voice was starting to rise. The bass player, without a shirt, limped out of a crusted-over bathroom, rubbing his nose. He glanced briefly in our direction, then at Margo.

"I gotta go now, Jimmy," she said.

"All right, all right, Babe, I don't have time to talk to you about it now." He started to trot around in circles. "I gotta get dressed, I gotta get dressed, you know I gotta play tonight. I gotta go." He threw on a wrinkled shirt and started to search wildly for his other sandal.

"Get your things, Margo."

"I don't have anything."

"Where's your clothes and makeup?"

Margo looked away and shrugged. "Oh, wait. I gotta take my pie." Then she ran into the kitchen and grabbed a crumbly, store-bought cherry pie and rushed past us to the car, without another glance at the bass player, who was ripping up the bedroom now.

"Throw that pie out." Margo's sister slammed the car door hard. "It stinks. We'll stop and buy some pizza."

"No, I need this pie."

Margo held on tightly to the pie, which had turned blue with mold, until we got to Idaho. No one could convince her that she wouldn't need it. "No, I'll get hungry if I throw it away." She held it on her lap even in the restaurants and truck stops we ate in.

It took us a couple months to get Margo through her withdrawal. Heroin was too hard to get in Idaho. But now she still had to stay pumped full of downers to stand it. Once in a while I'd see a flash of the old Margo, but she was pretty wrecked. We never talked about heroin, or Karon, or the L.A. jail. Both of us were so twisted up inside that we didn't talk much about anything anymore. We just got stoned. Sometimes I wanted to reach out and hug her tight and say "Margo, Margo, let's go away," but I knew she'd just think I was crazy; and besides, where could we go?

I frowned at her now as she ordered another drink, and that old feeling of helplessness washed over me again, but less intense, no doubt dulled by the tequila; so I ordered another drink, too. But before I had time to pour salt on my hand, I saw Greg walking across the dance floor towards us. My mouth dropped open, it seemed so funny to see him there. He worked in Alaska. He was supposed to be up north running by the side of dog sleds.

"Mind if I sit?" His voice was still velvety, low in his throat. I moved the chair back for him.

"What are you doing home?" Seeing him was like seeing a part of the past walk out of a dark closet. We'd gone to high school together, and he'd dated Karon quite a bit; but he'd left for Alaska a couple years ago, and now he worked there promoting bands. The night that he'd left, we'd thrown a big party on Tailor Mountain. I remember I'd been railing against the Viet Nam war and materialism and the food shortage in India, and he'd said, "If you want to change the world, you have to get on the level that change is made."

"And where's that?"

"Get as much money as Chevron or IBM, then you can move."

"And is that what you're going to do?" I'd asked him in disgust.

I could tell now by the way he dressed—quietly, expensively—that he must be making a lot of money in Alaska. I could also tell by his eyes that he wasn't into hard drugs. He sat back in his chair and studied me, and all of a sudden I became aware of my broken finger nails and limp hair.

"I just came home for a visit." He leaned forward. "How are *you* doing?" He wasn't going to mention Karon, though he'd heard, and I felt relieved.

"Great, I'm just great. You're sure looking good. Alaska must agree with you. Have you met Margo?" I nudged her, and she slowly bobbed her head upward until it was high enough to see Greg.

David came over on his break to talk to Greg, and we all agreed to go to the Westbank Hotel's dining room for breakfast at closing time. But by one o'clock my lips and cheeks were so numb that I could barely talk. Greg helped me into his car, and Margo and David followed in David's van. After we'd pulled out of the lighted downtown section, Greg reached under the front seat for a lid of grass. "Here, roll us one. Okay?"

But I spilled the papers all over my lap and the front seat, until he pulled down a side street and took the wrappings from me. Expertly rolling the joint, he said, "Hey, did you know you don't look so good?" His voice rolled in from a long way off as I nodded, fascinated with his hands as they sifted grass into the cigarette paper.

"What are you doing now, anyway?" he asked.

"Nothing."

"Is every night like this?"

"Yeah." It was hours since he had started rolling the joint. It grew rounder and slid in a slow, slow, liquid motion. I rolled down the window. Greg licked the end papers and stuck it in his mouth, leaning forward to push in the lighter.

"Do you know what I think you're doing?"

I turned my head back to look at him; I was interested. Could anyone really see me behind these clouds of pills and smoke? "No, what?"

"I think you're trying to follow Karon—right into the grave." He turned and looked straight at me.

I don't remember much after that, except that I felt I had to get out of his car right away. But we were driving now. I pushed my shoulder up tight against the door, ready to run as soon as we stopped; all I could think about was escape. But somehow I was able to restrain myself enough to walk tightly beside Greg into the cafe. He didn't speak to me again, though I was aware of him sadly watching my face through breakfast. David did most of the talking. Soon I excused myself to go to the bathroom and crept out the back door to walk home by the river. I didn't ever want to see Greg again. Who did he think he was? What right did he have talking to me like that? What did he know anyway, busy up there in the north, making all that money under the northern lights?

There was very little traffic now, and I could hear only the sound of moving water. My legs shook so badly that it was hard to walk on the graveled road. I felt as if an electric shock had been applied directly to my bones, and I could even taste the feeling of fear in my mouth. Images of Karon lying in her coffin flashed through my mind—her empty face, her stiff hands. Half of me lying on white satin; Dad standing in the background; Becky crying. I'd never been back to her grave after the funeral. Our twinness had been too complete, so that it would have been as if I were looking at my face and my brain and my legs, instead of hers, buried under the heavy, suffocating dirt. And she'd unfairly taken the best part of me and left behind the dregs. If I'd known, if I'd been better prepared, I could have withdrawn myself from her enough to stand alone. But instead, the ripping and tearing and wrenching of my own body was still going on, and the pain was so great that I tried to drown it, cover it, disguise it—nightly.

Spasms of uncontrolled emotion shook through me so much that I finally had to sit down in the tall grass by the road to calm down. The dark water moved sluggishly. Across the river, sitting on the opposite bank, was the LDS temple, all lit up like a bride before her wedding. Somewhere crickets started chirping, or had they been singing all along and I just now heard them? For a long time I lay back in the wet grass, waiting for the spasms to leave my arms and legs, watching the temple lights play on the river. Then, slipping off my sandals, I eased into the water and waded out chest-deep. I gasped for air against the coldness, rolling over on my back to stroke slowly parallel to the shore, staying away from the dangerous current in the middle. Cars sped by overhead on John Hole's bridge.

As kids we used to take turns diving from that bridge, but that was before they chopped off its antique top and streamlined it into a smooth concrete wonder. I could still hear the laughter and summer-afternoon yelling. I remember the adrenaline screaming in my stomach before each dive, making me feel as if I had to go to the bathroom. Climbing clear to the top, hand over hand, took enough time to allow for second thoughts. The sun beat hot on my shoulder, and the metal burned under my hands and feet. From the top of the bridge, the river below looked darker and faster—unfriendly and flat like a mirror. But we had to dive; there was no getting out of it. Everyone was watching. It was impossible for anyone to climb back down the bridge once he'd climbed to the top. The highest rail was a commitment to jump into the Snake. But one time at the top, just as I leaned forward to dive, my foot slipped; and my face hit the river at a weird angle. The slamming pain took my breath away, and the next thing I knew, Greg was dragging me up on the grass. A black bruise that turned blue, then yellow, covered the left side of my face for two weeks, and I never climbed to the top of the bridge again. It wasn't worth it—so much pain for such a little thrill.

I rolled over on my stomach, used to the cold now, and let my body slowly sink under the black water. The wetness crept up the back of my neck, heavy in my hair, until I was completely submerged. It shut off my sight, and closed my mouth and filled my ears and nose, and the dark oblivion felt good and sweet, wrapping me tight as the river swirled over my head and around my body.

But then I was wading towards shore. Moss pulled through my toes, and tiny rocks slipped underfoot. The river was gentle tonight. I climbed up the bank, tried to wring my shirt out, and smoothed my hair back tightly, away from my face. A car's lights flashed across the grass as it turned onto the freeway. A dog barked, and music from somewhere near the temple—probably a radio, maybe someone playing a guitar—floated across the dark water. With a deep breath I started the climb to the bridge, brushing through weeds and thistles. The steep grade was difficult, and my feet slipped on loose gravel several times, making me slide a way back down the hill until I could grab hold of a bush or small scrub tree. But in the dark the bush would often be a patch of thistles, and my arms and hands began to sting and bleed. Burrs clung to my pants and shirt as I scrambled over the rocks.

I finally reached the lighted concrete top of the bridge. Crawling under a high, barbed-wire fence, I sat on the railing and looked back at the dark water. It kept moving, unchanged by me. The river would go on forever, or at least until the earth ended, oblivious of my fears, unconcerned over dead sisters, swirling along the channel it had chosen— big, dark, forever moving. I sat still, a small wet bunch of rags on a bridge, knowing that Karon was really the only one who could understand. And she was gone. *Then who am I,* I wondered, *and where am I going?* The question echoed off the black river like a gunshot, bouncing off the dark houses, hitting the trees, ricocheting off the pavement, so loud and lonely I was sure that the furthest star had heard.

Jumping off the railing onto the road, I zigzagged between cars to cross over to the temple side of the river, and sloshed my way home in muddy sandals. But it was a long way home.

8

Come to Moscow

I needed in the worst way to talk to some-
one. I needed to talk so badly that the back of my throat was
tight with wanting to utter even the smallest syllable: "Hi,
how are you? No, I mean, really, how *are* you?"—anything
to stop the roaring isolated vacuum.

As I walked down Thirteenth South to the laundromat, I
searched every passing face for some opening, no matter how
small, some sign of approachability.

I'd been in Salt Lake City two weeks now, having come
from Denver; maybe subconsciously I was slowly easing towards Idaho again, towards home. I didn't know. I had
friends here I'd meant to look up the first night I got into
town. But each day I pushed actually calling them further
away from me, back into a corner of the little one-room
studio I'd rented. There, along with my books, on a piece of
paper entitled Notes to Myself, lay my good intentions.
Somehow I couldn't face my friends with my brains
splattered the way they were. I was ashamed that I wasn't
more together.

The laundromat was stuffy in the August heat. I pushed the coins hard into the washer slots. Machines were the enemy and were always trying to eat my money. Sitting on an orange vinyl couch against the window, I counted the bills left in my purse. I'd have to look for another waitress job soon, but for right now I had enough from my job in Denver to last another couple weeks. Waitressing was usually safe. I could normally handle taking an order for eggs.

"Toast or hashbrowns, sir?" But if a customer once broke the restaurant lingo and asked what my name was or where I was from, I was lost, floundering like a big fish belly-up on the beach. Not from drugs or alcohol. I'd quit them several months ago. But it didn't seem to matter. I still felt stoned and sank deeper into myself each day. Sometimes I was even unable to hear the talking around me or the traffic; then suddenly it would blare across my conscious mind as if someone had just turned on a giant tape recorder. "Now hear this! Now hear this!" and then the noise of the city screamed so loud and raw that I'd run back to my cramped room and sit on the floor by the radiator, hugging my knees tightly until my heart quit thumping at the sky.

Sometimes if I sat still long enough, the roaring pain would seep away slowly into sleep, the most blessed of all states, and I'd be able to float away from myself for a while, waking to watch the sunlight sliding down the faded wallpaper, the shadows easing out of the corners to fill the room, corresponding to the shadows inside me. Then I'd sit very still in the dark, hoping to hold onto the small island of quiet, mistaking an empty void for peace.

At other times the longer I sat, the worse the pain got. Crushing and swirling like some violent sea, it threatened to break through my skin and wash over the floor. I'd hug my legs tightly, burying my head against my knees, waiting for the end of the world—wishing for a quick gunshot through the head, welcoming a carelessly dropped atomic bomb, or at the very least an apartment fire that allowed everyone to escape but me (and my books), that would burn up the pain in a huge funeral bier reaching like Dido's to blacken the sky. And sometimes, like King Arthur in *Camelot,* I'd whisper and plead, "Merlin, Merlin, fly me away from here. Fly me away."

In Denver I'd worked with a Jewish boy who talked day and night about the coming Messiah. He washed dishes in the back and always took his lunch break the same time I did. I liked Eric, with his thick black hair and jerky walk, even though he was wound too tightly most of the time. He was like a big, raised fist. "You wait—he's coming," he'd say as he shook a fork of mashed potatoes at me. "And he'll clean up this mess. The Messiah is coming." He'd thrust his perspiring face close to mine and whisper, "He'll save us." Then he'd jump up to go back to work as if someone on the ceiling had yanked him suddenly with a stiff rope. Eric hated bosses, cops, army men, and presidents. It took me a while to understand that it was fear that fed his hatred, a deeply rooted paranoia about the world around him. And each newspaper headline, every radio broadcast, intensified his terror.

I really wanted to believe that a Messiah was on his way. Sometimes after work I'd sit on the step of the apartment building, watching people, waiting for the sun to go down, and I'd let my mind slide to rest on an image of the Messiah, dressed in white robes, coming down from the clouds, light streaming from his face in all directions. It felt good to dream about the Savior, but Eric was sort of crazy. He didn't show up for work sometimes and often forgot to comb his hair.

Yet, now in Salt Lake City, I still waited like Eric for the Messiah, waited for Merlin, for my fairy godmother, guardian angel, for Santa Claus, Superman—anyone would do, anyone who had a clearer vision than I did, anyone who knew, who spoke truth. But though I waited, I had no hope. Unlike Eric, I didn't believe anymore even in the simplest things. If the sun had failed to rise some morning, I would not have been surprised. If the pavement had shifted suddenly under my feet, I would not have lifted an eyebrow.

All the washers across from me were full now, and the sound of wet clothes swishing back and forth was making me slightly drowsy. I turned on the vinyl couch and pressed my forehead against the cool window pane, wishing I could stop thinking for a while, put my mind on hold. Just then my eyes focused on a girl climbing out of a blue car. Very pregnant, she set a large load of wash down on the pavement, then she reached for two small children in the back seat. There was something vaguely familiar about her. I turned slightly on the couch to watch her hold the door open for the kids before she went back to get the wash. I knew her. It was Mary Ann Campbell, a girl from my high school class. Mary Ann. Pretty and popular, house on the hill, all her dental work done by age thirteen. How I'd always envied her then—and how I envied her now, because she had two beautiful kids and I could tell she was straight.

Mary Ann was having trouble in lifting the wash to a table, and I was just about to go help her when she turned around and cuffed the smaller boy, who was whining for ice cream. She pushed the little girl towards him. "Take Matt and go sit down and don't you move until I tell you to." Then she smiled at the lady next to her and began complaining about the heat. "Oh, do you always use that kind of spray and wash?" she asked the lady. "I used to use that kind, but I'm not kidding, this stuff is so much better." She held up a green spray bottle. "I was so disappointed in the kind you're using that I almost wrote the company to protest." She went on and on, just like a commercial. I could have walked over and flipped a button, and the channel would have changed to Mary Ann advertising soda pop or bleach or shampoo.

Her kids had come over to climb on the bench next to me. "Do you have any gum?" the little girl asked. I shook my head shyly.

"Stop bothering people," Mary Ann yelled from across the washers, and for a few seconds our eyes met. My breath almost stopped in anticipation of talking with her, but she didn't recognize me. Had it been that long? Only four years. Had I changed so much? But then I remembered my long braided hair and faded Levi's, and I realized that all Mary Ann saw was another burnt-out hippie who didn't have any gum for her kids.

All at once the air in the laundromat seemed suffocating. I jumped up and ran for the door, which seemed almost too heavy to open, not waiting for my clothes to dry, not caring. I turned west and walked as fast as I could for several blocks, stopping finally at a water fountain. I was so thirsty, but the fountain was dry, caked with mud in the middle. I walked more slowly now, heading west again directly into the setting sun, feeling nothing but my feet hitting the pavement and a great thirst.

I thought of the tiny china swan that had fallen from Karon's hands and broken on my grandmother's floor. Grandma called it an heirloom, a treasure because it was a link to her past. But then when we couldn't glue it back together, Grandma said Karon could now be the china swan for Grandma—a great treasure linking her to the future.

But Karon had broken and bled all over the floor.

I walked past shop doors and restaurants and crowds of people going home from work, not really knowing or caring where I was going until I stood before a black wrought-iron gate with a sign that said Visitors Welcome. Temple Square, the Mormon Temple surrounded by cascading flowers and fountains and green, green lawns. I remembered hearing someone say once that they were sure Mormons worshipped seagulls because of all the statues of birds on the temple grounds. But it looked cool and clean and ordered inside, and I could see a water fountain. Then I was pushing open a glass door to the visitors center, and I drank from a brown water fountain just inside the door. I felt so dehydrated, so dried out, that gallons and gallons of water didn't seem enough. I finally collapsed on a bench against the window.

Maybe I sat for hours, maybe only minutes, I don't know. It was very quiet, although there were many people. I sat still, not wanting to move even a small finger, because I felt so strange, as if someone was holding me close and gently stroking my hair. The sensation was so comfortable and so new that I wanted to turn into a mannequin there on the bench so I wouldn't have to leave when they locked up the doors. I hushed even my breathing and slowly looked around. Where was I? I watched several groups of tourists stop in front of the wall paintings on the other side of the room, and finally I stood to wander after them, down the reddish-brown carpet, past the lighted paintings of men thinking deeply, wondering, listening, and praying. I looked at each one long and carefully, as if I could soak up the colors and the peace. Or was the peace in the room, not in the paintings, but in the air around the paintings?

Then I walked upward into the blue room with white and pink clouds painted along the walls, wide windows, and a blue bench—an empty room except for a white sculpture of the Savior, his hands outstretched as if blessing someone, nail slashes in the palms and feet. Planets and stars swirled around his head on the wall behind him. Out of the window to the right was the great stone temple with spires pointing straight up towards the sky. "It's a pretty church, isn't it?" a lady said behind my shoulder. "It's not a church," her husband said softly. "It's a temple."

The room was very quiet, though a steady flow of people walked past the statue, which seemed bigger than it really was. Many stared for a long time at the great calm in the face, moving away slowly, almost reluctantly, to follow after their children, who were eager to climb the next set of stairs. The statue looked like the pictures of Jesus that our Primary teacher used to stick on her flannel board. *Is this what the ruler of the universe looks like?* I thought. *A wandering Jew?*

Then I walked by myself around a circle where there were no people and sat on a bench against the wall. A security guard passed by, eyeing me cautiously. After he was gone I saw in the middle of the other wall, paintings of the crucifixion: the Savior nailed to the middle cross, blood oozing from feet and hands, his body bunched with pain, women kneeling, crying at his feet. A tour group of people passed by the painting led by a slightly nervous young man in a blue suit. He talked briefly—too briefly—about the Atonement, moving along quickly with an old man wearing red suspenders, a young girl in culottes and a sleeveless blouse, small children scratching their arms, and a fidgety older lady in bulging pink pants. I could smell wintergreen mints on someone's breath. Then a young girl with white barrettes in her hair read the inscription under the painting: "But he was wounded for our transgressions, he was bruised for our iniquities; the chastisement of our peace was upon him; and with his stripes we are healed." They moved on, the words hanging in the air behind them. Then I heard only the muted sound of air-conditioning and faraway talking. I wished I could curl up on the soft bench in front of the paintings—at the feet of the Savior—and sleep, maybe forever. But it was his face that got to me—I couldn't stop looking at his face.

Mary Ann, shallow Mary Ann. Shame on you for babbling about laundry soap when the sun could fall from the sky tomorrow. Don't you know that the battle is bloody? I thought of other faces, friends I'd loved, those who had sat on the riverbanks with me and discussed the Milky Way.

Tom and Kent—the clowns. In his rumbling blue jeep Tom often came to get me on his lunch hour. He'd drive into the country, where we'd lie in the summer breeze and eat avocado sandwiches and watermelon. If there was a dance or a party, Tom made sure that I had a ride even if he had an important date for the evening. He was more like a brother than a real blood-brother.

And Kent, crazy and unpredictable, made us laugh as he balanced cans of beer on his head while he tried to cross the river on a log bridge, like a tightrope walker. Tom and Kent were mad, and so electric they lit up every street they walked down.

One night they raced a train and the train won, smashing into the driver's side of the car. Kent's neck snapped in two; the bottle between his legs didn't even break. In fact he barely bled, but he died. Tom's eyes were glazed over when they wheeled him into the emergency room, but he lived.

With a huge metal plate holding his brains together, he still babbles and slobbers his way around his dad's farm.

And Cheryl, olive-skinned Cheryl; compared to Mary Ann she shone like a goddess in my mind—as much a sister as my twin. The drug world threatened to turn either her brains or her inside out. Drugs had already cost her a marriage. Finally, filled with panic, she left town with her small son, moving to Phoenix, Arizona, to work in a restaurant.

One summer she fished the limp body of her beautiful son out of a friend's swimming pool. At the funeral she stood by the casket instead of in the line to receive people. And when the funeral director approached to shut the coffin, she dug her fingernails deep into my arm and whispered, "Help me, I'm going to scream."

"No, you're fine, easy now, easy," I crooned as I would to a trembling colt, smoothing her long hair back from her face. But I wanted to scream, too.

And ethereal, mystical Nick who searched for God through Yellowstone Park and an Indian reservation. He'd lived in six foster homes before he turned twelve. Once I called his house to tell him we'd be right over, and his mother blew fire through the receiver. "He's the devil! He's possessed. I threw him out," she screamed. "And I'll call the cops if he ever comes near here again." Later we found Nick walking by the river, and he never said a word, except to ask us if we'd go with him to the city zoo to buy some popcorn. One of his dreams was to someday unlock the cages and let all those neurotic animals loose. Sweet Nick, dying with a silver spoon on cold bathroom tile in the first year of his marriage.

I saw my sister's face. Shy and timid Karon, who would bleed for days over hurting someone's feelings.

I saw another friend named Todd who tried to join the Mormon church. While he was attending Ricks College and in a drug rehabilitation program, he came over one night to eat fresh strawberries with us. We sat on the floor and listened a long time to his Mormon doctrine. "We'll be gods someday. You can't go much higher than that. And another thing—we actually chose to come to this world. I'm not kidding, we shouted for joy." It sounded good to us.

The next week the newspaper carried the story of Todd's arrest. He'd broken into a Rexburg drugstore, shot drugs into both arms, then loaded a rifle and blasted the inside walls apart. Two years later, on his first weekend home from prison, he borrowed Neil's truck and shot up one last, deliberate time. Neil found the truck the next morning in a parking lot with Todd lying across the front seat, the tape deck still blaring out Santana.

Other faces floated into view. Many of the 116th Battalion of Engineers had been my high school friends, my midnight swimming buddies, my barroom dancing partners. When they came home from Viet Nam, the local television cameras were at the airport. I watched them on the screen climbing off the plane. Like animals coming out of a tunnel into bright sun, they moved too slowly, no feeling on their faces, staring back at the cameras. I knew that vacant look, those apathetic muscles that meant drugs, and lots of them. They meant living too long with something dead. They meant an unhealthy resignation after too much horror, too much insanity. My insides squeezed down hard as I watched the group bunch together, standing back from friends and family.

The sixties, the waste—almost a whole generation. Nothing wrong with us except that maybe we'd burned too bright in the wrong decade. Timing. Had it all been timing?

I looked up again at the painting, the weeping women, the Savior's head hanging to one side. And the tears came—for myself, for my family, for my beautiful friends, for him. And it was very dark though the aisle was well lit.

Father, we have paid too—for our stupidity, our blindness. To the sounds of Joplin and Hendrix, we have bled, too.

And with his stripes we are healed.

And suddenly I was praying—praying intensely, feverishly, to the childhood God I'd learned about in Primary.

Dear Father,

I probably do not deserve to even say your name.

I don't even know for sure if you're there.
But if it is true that you exist and rule over things, could
you tell me?
If you have the power to create the universe
and organize everything in it,
then you have the power to let me know about you.
And though I am in the middle of great sin and trouble,
I plead with you to hear my prayer.
Would you help me to live,
to even want to live.
For I am tired and dying.

And that is where it started. Or maybe it began the day I
was born, or the day Karon died. I don't know. But I actually
felt the beginnings that day at Temple Square—slowly, flut-
tering like tiny moth wings at first, flickering, a tiny spark.
Then, over time, more sure as the knowing came in incre-
ments, like a solemn unveiling in the deepest part of me.

I read—book after book after book: the Old Testament,
the New Testament, the Book of Mormon. I started with an
old Sunday School manual called *Christ's Ideals for Living*
that I bought for twenty-five cents at a curio shop that same
day on the way home from Temple Square. And certain scriptures stood out like neon signs blazing across the sky. "Come
unto me . . . and I will give you rest." "Trust in the Lord with
all thine heart; and lean not unto thine own understanding."

And along with the words came delicate feelings, astound-
ing feelings. It was as though I was being tutored by God himself. The words moved in me like hot stew on a cold and hungry night. And the crust around my body cracked and broke
open in places and began to fall away, allowing me to breathe
and to see and to feel such things as wind on my face and
water running through my hands.

One day I called a friend in Moscow, Idaho, who I knew
had joined the Church.

"Come to Moscow," she said. "Salt Lake is too hot in the
summer." So I closed the door on my small apartment that

was so much like a coffin and left for Northern Idaho, for sky and rolling hills and pine trees.

The night I arrived she took me with her to a family home evening, and I sweated my way through it until the refreshments came. I felt so out of place and uncomfortable that I couldn't wait to escape into the night outside again. I was too numb. The oatmeal cookies stuck in my throat, and I stumbled over my good-byes. I was not interested in people, only in getting closer to God. And I did not yet associate the two. I was like a small child trying to find ways to crawl onto her father's lap, almost desperate for his closeness.

But I continued to read, and the words were sweet. Soon I moved into a place of my own where the words surrounded me, bouncing off the walls and ceilings, greeting me in the morning and putting me to bed at night. And I wanted them to be true. I believed in God now, the same God who fed the children of Israel with manna that they might not perish in the wilderness. Where else could these feelings be coming from? I wasn't generating them inside myself, for my brain and soul had been as dead and still as cement for a long time now. And the feelings were real and very physical.

But still I fought against the idea of the LDS Church, although I could not seem to go anywhere without running into LDS missionaries. There was only one chapel in Moscow, but it seemed to have about a thousand missionaries, because they were everywhere, even sitting in the cafes I went to and buying groceries next to me at the local store. Coincidence? I was beginning to doubt it. Yet I had searched and studied so many systems and ideas that it was difficult for me to imagine that the religion of my childhood, of my ancestors, could be the plan, the pearl, of the universe. Besides, it would be a very narrow gate for me to walk through. I had lived far away from the teachings of the Church for a long time.

"You need to talk to the bishop now," my friend said.

"What would I say?"

"You'll know."

So she made an appointment with the bishop for me as

you would with a doctor. He was a professor of speech at the university, a mild man who must have wondered what he'd got himself into when he saw me. I was pretty burnt and looked it.

"Well, let's see if you belong in this ward first."

Immediately I saw his reluctance and withdrew myself from him. What could he say anyway? He was only a man.

He talked on and on, vague words that didn't connect with me, while I waited for a decent time to pass before I could excuse myself. But then I realized he was waiting for me to speak; not only him but many others were waiting unseen. It was as if the sky and trees outside waited breathlessly, too. And the silence was thick and intense. They kept waiting. For what? I twisted uncomfortably against a gush of words that rose in my throat. He leaned forward in his chair and said, "I am your bishop. Is there something you wanted to tell me?"

"No, I don't think so." But all at once I was telling him everything—confessing, from the beginning, though I knew nothing of the law of confession. When I had finished, he sat very still, heavy in his chair, looking at his hands.

I sat across from him, surprised—in fact, stunned—over the ugly bare words that still hung in the air.

"I don't know why I told you all that. I really don't even know why I'm here," I said, nervously rubbing my hands together.

A great silence filled the room. The bishop was deep in thought; then he spoke. "There's a scripture that says, 'My sheep know my voice.'" Tears filled his eyes. He seemed touched by some unknown presence, and he struggled to speak through waves of deep emotion.

Just then someone knocked at the door. We both sat very still, unwilling to break the peace that was so tangible it seemed to press against our skin. But the person knocked again, and the bishop shrugged off slight irritation and opened the door. The institute director and a student apologized for their intrusion and riffled through some papers on a table by the door. The bishop stood politely by them; maybe he felt a little afraid that the intrusion would chase away what was building in that room. But I saw it as a reprieve, a break for me to see for myself what was going on. And I looked around the cluttered office in wonder.

There *was* something different. The tacky prints on the wall, hung too high, didn't look so tacky any longer. They simply seemed a soft reflection of the man. Pictures of his family—at a picnic, swimming, standing around a table—stood on a dusty shelf behind a piled desk. Rain ran in jagged patterns down the window, drops swirling around the dirt crusted on the outside of the pane. It was by far the most peaceful room I'd ever been in.

The two intruders left, too soon for me, and the bishop returned to his seat. He looked at me intently and said, "You must judge. The Savior's real and very much alive. Don't lose his voice among the chaos of your mind."

I nodded. I knew what he meant.

Then the bishop reached out and patted my hand. "It is time for you to come home."

And so I came back. And the next few years I slowly fought to bring my body in tune with the strict laws of the Church. I learned about the process of repentance and felt it crushing and moving and burning and cleaning within me. I remember lying on a bed, sweating and crying as I realized the depth of the pain I had caused others. Those days and months were excruciating. Yet hope was pulsing through every hour. As a new child screams through a narrow passage into the world, I fought through it a day at a time. It was very dark, and then it wasn't.

And then I dreamt that we were leaving a chapel after sacrament meeting to attend Sunday School. There would be three classes taught that day: the telestial, the terrestrial, and the celestial. Of course, we thought, we will attend the class teaching of the highest kingdom. But as we moved down the hall we passed the open door of the telestial class, and we saw many of our friends inside. Also, teaching the class was our favorite teacher. We paused for a few minutes to look in and heard him say, "Today we will learn about telestial principles such as how to pay bills, unclog sinks, and plant apple trees." For some reason we were fascinated, and we moved in to join our friends, feeling that there was plenty of time left to attend the celestial class.

Then I had another dream, and in it everything I had lost or thrown away was returned. My flesh came together again, whole and complete. And a woman washed me and placed small white slippers on my feet and a veil on my hair, and led me up a polished wood staircase, worn smooth by many hands, to a white room with much sun, and in the middle of the room was a beautifully carved wooden chair. The chair still rocked slightly as if the mother who had sat waiting had left the room only seconds before, and I felt sure it would be only seconds until her return. How I longed for her return!

So it began. I came back to my heritage, and I learned that only strangers travel and seek for signs of God in the landscape. I came home again and was surprised to find lying right in front of me the richness and harmony I'd been searching for. It had been there all along. Mormonism was not only true but delightful. And it was good to be home.

9

In Times of Trouble

As I walked through the front door at two minutes to six, I saw her leaning against the back wall, one arm crossed over her waist, the other resting upon it, a cigarette burning in her hand. I silently vowed that she wasn't going to get to me tonight. No matter what Donna the Whip did or said, she wasn't going to upset me.

I stopped long enough at the cash register to log in and pick up my ticket book.

"How's school going?" Sally asked.

"Pretty good. It's been a long week, though. Think we'll have a big bar-run tonight?" I hated bar-runs: a mad rush of people pouring through the doors after the bars downtown closed. The crowd was usually loud and often obnoxious, as well as headachy, ornery, and sloppy. They came in all at once and exited all at once, leaving behind spilled cream and sugar, smeared food on the tables, overturned napkin holders, and piles and piles of dirty dishes.

"Maybe," Sally said while filing down her little fingernail. "We've been pretty busy so far."

I'd been lucky to land this job on weekends. The money I made at the cafe plus the money from my job during the week at the library was really helping me through school. I had to keep telling myself that so the tiredness didn't have a chance to creep up my spine.

"Hello, Donna," I said as I passed her, trying to muster a smile.

"Hello," she mumbled as she reached for her coffee cup sitting on a shelf beside her.

Donna was a puzzle. Bitter and brittle, she snapped at the world like a trapped fox. Yet she usually counted out more tips at the end of the night's work than anyone else. I'd watch her laugh and flirt with her customers as though she had all the time in the world. But the minute she hit the waitress station in the back, everyone got out of her way. Though she never spoke to us except to complain or to insult, we felt her presence constantly like a sour dishrag stuffed under our noses. I'd never met anyone who hated so many things, and I always dreaded working with her. By the end of the shift I was usually so drained that I barely had the energy to go home and wash the smoke and grease out of my hair.

This weekend I'd drawn double duty with her, and I felt sick over it. Not because I was afraid of her, but because I was tired, and when I was this tired, her bitterness seemed to rub my skin like a bar of lye soap. But it couldn't be helped. I'd just have to ignore her, I thought, as I leaned up against the wall beside her to study the night's menu.

Just then Lucy, my small, wrinkled Japanese boss, came padding down the aisle carrying her ledger book, nodding to customers on the right and left like a wound-up oriental doll. When she saw me, her face lit up with mischief. Lucy was an old-time practical joker, and I wondered what was up her sleeve now.

"Oh, hello," she bubbled. "How was your week? You work so hard. So, do you know what? I bought you a rare kind of chocolate for a treat. Here, I've kept it in the back of the fridge all week so it wouldn't melt." She straightened up from reaching into the back of the refrigerator and handed me a brightly-wrapped square of chocolate.

"Oh, yeah, sure," snorted Donna out of the side of her mouth. "Real treat. It's a chocolate-covered bee."

Lucy's face fell. And I had to laugh out loud. Her good humor always returned quickly, but she glared hard at Donna as she passed her on the way to the kitchen, where I heard her throw Japanese at the salad boy.

She was a good woman and made working at the cafe bearable for me. College was taking so long and seemed so hard. Maybe because I had never finished high school; I didn't even stay long enough to learn basics, which made me have to double-time now. I'd received high enough scores on my ACT that they'd let me enter Ricks Junior College without a diploma. Then Lucy had offered me this job during Christmas break and I'd jumped at the chance, staying on after the season to work weekends. Because she made me laugh, I didn't mind the grease and smoke so much. One night a boy left me a twenty-dollar bill for a cup of coffee.

But I did mind working with Donna. She was so endlessly and intensely bitter that I couldn't stay above it for long. And soon I'd be thinking of all the crummy things in my own life, too; which really was absurd, since I'd had so many blessings lately. With each day that passed, I was feeling more and more like a Latter-day Saint, and had even cleaned up my life to the point at which I could look forward to entering the temple one day—the beautiful, sacred temple.

"You'd better get that coffee made," Donna yelled over her shoulder. "I'm not about to make it anymore tonight. I've had my fill of it the last four nights."

Well, that's really fair, Donna, I thought. *I wasn't anywhere near here the last four nights, but I get to pay for your trouble.* I poured myself a Seven-up and tried to clear my head of homework assignments long enough to adjust to an eight-hour shift.

And it was a long, long shift, much longer than eight hours —it seemed at least forty-eight hours. One of the cooks got mad at Sally for calling in a take-out order during the dinner rush and threw a pan of fried rice against the wall. Of course, Sally and I cleaned it up to avoid any more trouble. Then a customer at one of my tables sent back her steak three different times for three different reasons. The day-shift girls had forgotten to fill the creamers and sugar bowls, and we didn't notice it until we were swamped with customers, all screaming for fresh cream for their coffee. The salad boy dropped a whole bucket of ice near the coffee machine, and it was remarkable that one of us didn't break her neck trying to work around it until he found the mop, which was upstairs behind some boxes in the bathroom. Tips were lousy, customers were rude, and I was exhausted before I even began. And, of course, there was Donna with her barbs and switchblade knives.

During the bar-run, it got even worse. Jeff Burrows, a regular, came in sloppy drunk and fell face first into his bowl of noodles. After cleaning him up, we called a cab. Then Ken and Rick started a brawl near the cash register, which brought both cooks screaming from the kitchen (secretly glad for any kind of break in their routine).

Then, fifteen minutes before closing time, I seared the whole back of my hand with hot coffee. Unable to hold tears of frustration any longer, I let loose with several four-letter words from my past, just as Donna was walking by with an order.

"Oh my," she said gleefully. "Listen to our little reformed Mormon. Did you learn that in Sunday class?"

My heart sank. I really was a fine example, wasn't I? It hurt. Trying to prepare for a temple recommend, and I couldn't even keep my mouth clean. I bit down hard on the tears until we were finished with the clean-up work, then hurried out to the car, not even stopping to cash in my tips. Then the tears came, a whole week's worth—heaves and gushes. I was so tired!

On the way home, I turned left towards the river, trying to get control. Soon I found myself parked in front of the

Idaho Falls Temple. The lights around the white marble blurred and swam before me, until I dropped my head on the steering wheel and sobbed again. It seemed as if all the months of uphill fighting and frustration had piled up at once and come crashing down around my head. I found myself praying, drenched in self-pity: "I thought things would get better. Well, they're not better. Everything's hard. And where are you? Can't you help? I can't go back and work with her tomorrow. Can't you see I'm tired? I am so very tired." Then I cried even harder.

But suddenly I became aware of warmth in the car, though it was in the middle of winter and I had turned off the engine. Slowly my crying stopped and I leaned back, physically very comfortable, as if fitting into someone's arms. Across my mind flashed a line from my patriarchal blessing, which I had received the previous year: "The Lord has placed guardian angels around you to protect you, comfort you, and guide you, and in your times of trouble you will be able to feel their spirits near." I shifted in my seat, gazing at the whiteness of the temple.

Finally I sat still, looking at a tree on the grounds. It was a huge, drooping willow with snow clustered on its branches. Stars shone through the top part of the tree like a halo. And I remember thinking how wonderful to be planted as a tree on holy ground. The temple rose strong against the night, its spiral pointing toward heaven. Soft lights around its base played on wintered shrubs and frozen flowerbeds. Fresh snow mounded the marble benches placed here and there. As soon as April came, couples would stroll among the flowers, stopping to sit underneath the willow trees and watch spring birds, feeling the wash of a slightly cool breeze promising summer. I'd seen them.

I loved the temple, though I had never been inside. Since I was a small child, I had been taught to respect and reverence the sacred covenants that one makes within its holy rooms. Inside, everyone dressed in white and spoke softly if they spoke at all. There was no mystery, no dark secrets, although

only certain members of the Church were allowed to enter—
those who were totally committed to following the Savior
and especially committed to loving. We were taught that no
hatred, no bitterness, no petty fears should cross the thresh-
old, or holy ground would be desecrated. Therefore, to enter
the temple took much preparation. The heart had to be clear,
soft, and forgiving. And in return one would be administered
to by angels. Inside those sacred walls was home.

Now the soft light from the temple windows poured out
onto the new snow promising peace. And all at once it hit me.
I realized that I had been given the greatest gift that mankind
could receive. It was not money, nor an education. It was not
even a companion and children. My greatest gift was my
knowledge of the Savior. I knew he was a reality, now and
forever. I knew this as surely as I knew my own name. And
suddenly, like a flash of clear, bright sunshine, I understood
that no matter what others believe, my testimony could lift
me to someday walk beyond the highest star.

The searing peace that followed this insight shook the
whole temple grounds.

I don't know how much longer I sat leaning over the
steering wheel. Even though I was still wide awake, I felt as if
my body had slept peacefully for hours on the softest bed.
The tiredness oozed out of my muscles, leaving my legs and
arms relaxed and still. Softly quiet. My mind rested comfort-
ably as though I had been sitting under a pine tree on a grassy
hill, gazing at a rippling lake below.

It didn't matter anymore that I stay parked near a temple. I
knew he could reach me anytime, anywhere. And I wanted to
be waiting.

Driving home I realized the roads were much icier than I'd
noticed before, but the snow hanging from trees and houses
glistened like fairy-dust in the cold. The night was beautiful.
Once home, I took a long, relaxing bubble bath before I set
up the ironing board to press a clean uniform for the next
day's work.

10

Rodeo Nights

A horse was killed that night, a palomino with a creamy-white mane and tail. He broke his neck, catching the audience off guard. We saw him rearing in the chutes, pawing at the top rails as the rider tried to ease down on his back. Then he split with rage as they opened the gate. Beautiful, insulted horseflesh. Bucking hard, he threw his rider quickly; then blinded by his fury, he smashed headfast into the wooden arena fence. The rodeo director immediately called in a tractor pulling a low platform, and a rope was tied around the horse's middle. He was hoisted onto the wooden plank, his legs dangling limp over the side. The crowd was quiet.

He'd died instantly. I'd heard the snap of his neck from where I sat in the grandstands with my son, my nephew, and my father. But a cowboy rode with the horse out of the arena, holding the horse's head on his lap to fool the crowd into thinking he was still alive, that he'd be all right later after they'd rubbed him down with oil or given him a shot or whatever they did to fix old, busted rodeo horses.

Death is a strange thing, and people react to it in different ways. Even the death of a horse can cause some people's stomachs to squeeze up tight, turn their thoughts away from rodeos to dwell on dark empty voids. The rodeo announcer rippled a joke through the microphone, drawing the clowns into absurd action to cover up the horse's death, and the rodeo went on.

We sat on hard, wooden benches, eating hamburgers and writing down each cowboy's riding score on the program. My father, an old man in faded Levi's and a felt cowboy hat, leaned back against the bench behind him. Most of the cowboys were friends of his, and he compared their performances tonight with other rides, other nights. When they got bored, the two little boys crawled through the bleachers to look for fallen money. They climbed back up between our legs again when the clowns brought out their gear for the bull riding: a dummy with red underwear, a big barrel, and huge rubber inner tubes to toss at a bull's head to draw his attention away from a hurt cowboy. Bull riding is the most dangerous event of a rodeo, but the clowns' silly, often crazy antics, combined vaudeville comedy with high drama.

We stayed long after the last event was over, and as we walked through the sagebrush to the car, I felt full with the sounds and smells of the summer night. There's nothing like amateur rodeos; they get in your blood. Crawling into the back of the car with a blanket, I let the two boys ride in the front with their grandfather and propped my feet up for the long drive to our summer cabin. As we drove I watched the moon through the window and felt warm and sleepy, as I used to when I was a little girl and the world was safe. Driving home from rodeos then was no different from now—except that this time, reflected in the glow from the car radio, was not a strong, young father, but an old man with a deeply-creased face and weathered hands. The rodeo had loosened his tongue, and he was telling the boys stories, and because he usually talked only in short, one-word sentences to the boys, they were listening intently. Their words drifted back to me through the hum of the old car.

"Which one was the best horse you ever owned, Grandpa?"

"Oh, I've had a lot of good ones, but the best all-round working horse I owned was probably a little buckskin pony I raised from a colt. Named him Buck, and he could work all day and not even break into a sweat."

"What happened to him? Did you sell him?"

"Well, no, right after your mother's sister died, I took him and another sorrel colt of mine up into the hills . . . ."

He didn't say he'd left to get away from the smell of coffins and heavy murmuring talk and women crying, but I knew. He'd nearly smothered under her death, which had left a gray, empty space in my mind, too, as if someone had skipped three or four lines in the middle of typing an important letter, and then had started again three-fourths of the way down the page. I missed her still, maybe even more now.

"Them ponies were good ones," my father's voice droned on in the front seat. "The sorrel was a three-year-old. Pretty thing. I broke her myself."

I remember being angry when Karon died, looking hard for someone or something to blame. I had even been angry with her, hating her for the shaking of my dad's hands when he drove to tell Mother. I'd never before, nor have I since, seen my father cry as he did that day—huge, heaving sobs that shut off his breathing. You could tell he didn't do it much because his crying was rough and gulping. He just couldn't get the words out across the space between him and my mother. They say the death of a child is even harder than the death of a sister.

"We was hauling them horses in a horse trailer behind that old blue truck of mine. Had our gear and grub in the back of the truck covered with a canvas to keep the dust and rain off it."

In the semi-dark, I saw the younger little boy's head drop

to one side and roll a little. He turned and nestled down to lean against my son, who was still tight with attention, his eyes on his grandfather's face.

"Well, we started climbing into the pines and that old blue truck coughed and spit real good to warm itself up. It was a fine day—not too warm, not too cool—just right for a long jaunt up over the divide. Ol' Buck, he was feeling good, too. Kept dancing around and pawing the side of that trailer. I swerved the truck a couple of times, trying to get his attention and make him stand straight. If a horse gets to moving around too much, he'll tip a rig over. But swerving didn't help none. Ol' Buck just kept tossing his head, smelling that air; he wanted out into that open country as bad as I did."

My father looked down at my son and smiled—not a flashy grin, but a slow, spreading smile that came from somewhere deep inside, reaching up to crinkle the leather furrows around his eyes. He shifted a little in his seat as he looked back to the road.

"Well, about then, the trailer hitch come undone," he said. "I never did find out why; maybe it was the way I hitched it up, or maybe it was just plumb wore out. When the tongue hit the ground, the trailer rolled, throwing both horses out. When I got back there, Buck was down—screaming—his eyes rolling white in his head. I'd speak to him and he'd paw the air with his front feet, scrambling to get up, but the back part of him wasn't moving."

My father's voice hadn't changed in tone at all. He was still talking quiet and easy, slow, as if out for a Sunday walk; but Jason and I were both leaning forward to catch his words. I shivered at the image of my father, having left town to get away from his daughter's death, standing now in the mountains talking softly to his favorite horse as he watched him fight his own dying.

"A guy came along in a jeep with a gun, and we shot Buck right there. The little sorrel colt was busted up pretty bad, but we got her in the truck and took her home. I thought maybe we could save her, but she was too bad off, and a couple days later she got down and didn't get back up."

We pulled to a stop at an intersection, and my father slowly rolled down the window, letting in the scent of new-cut hay.

"How did ya know to shoot him, Grandpa?" Tears were just behind Jason's voice. "Maybe he would've been all right if ya hadn't shot him."

"No, Son, his back was broken. When I took the saddle off, trying to ease him, I could see the jagged edge of the break. There's no cure for a broken back."

"Did ya shoot him yourself?"

"Naw, your ol' grandpa had to walk up the road while the guy with the jeep shot him. I was feeling a little sick."

As we turned down the road that led to the cabin, in the silence left from his words, I looked at my father and probably saw him for the first time in years. Here was a nail-hard cowboy who had herded sheep and cattle all over the mountains of Idaho and Montana; built roads during a war in Korea and killed snakes in the jungles of New Guinea; raised children and watched them die and raised horses to shoot them. And I wondered at his never blaming someone or something for that trailer hitch that slipped that day in the hills.

A few minutes later Jason and I walked back through the dark pine trees from the outhouse. Pine cones and dry sticks crunched under our feet. A branch pulled at my pant leg. We remembered to walk around the small hole Reggie had dug that morning for his army men.

"I feel so bad for Grandpa," Jason said quietly. "I can't stop thinking about his horses."

We leaned against the car to look at the stars before going inside. It was one of those nights when everything seems to be singing. My muscles ached a little from hiking that morning and from our afternoon swim. I slipped off my sandals—the dirt was still warm from the sun—and reached over to massage the back of Jason's neck. Way off a dog barked, and the sky held a million lights. Fireflies and moths buzzed around the yard light. Aspens, crickets, rustling water— everything seemed to play off everything else as if the single intent of the night were comfort and consolation.

"I know. But it's all right, Jason. It's all right with Grandpa, too, although it's hard to understand. It was bad, what he told you, but rodeo nights like this one, and you listening to him, and hot scones for breakfast and swimming in the lake tomorrow—all that makes shooting horses okay."

Jason was quiet, and I remembered my grandpa talking to me one evening a long time ago. Though I had not understood then, it had been good.

Crickets chirped and small things rustled in the bushes. We stood under those swaying pines, listening to night birds for a long time, letting the dark wash us clean for the next day.

11

An Unseen Presence

We drove to Idaho Falls for the funeral. It wasn't urgent that we go. She wasn't my mother or even my grandmother, just an aunt. And it wouldn't be a sad funeral. She'd been suffering from cancer for two years and had spent the last months shrinking into a skeleton. So it wasn't as if our coming would ease anyone's pain, because the real pain of losing her would come much later to my uncle and my cousins, after the Relief Society sisters had gone and the flowers and casseroles had stopped coming and the last of the thank-you notes had been written. Then the pain would come only from missing her, because they were strictly Mormon and knew she was now safely, even happily, waiting for them on the other side of the veil.

But I wanted to go home; I wanted to be there, even though I was heavily, painfully pregnant, and each of the last fifty miles in the cramped car made me swear that my husband and I would adopt from now on. I loved her very much and wanted our family to pay tribute to her, especially if she was watching from the other side.

Besides, I felt ashamed. The week before she had died, while I was sitting in my office correcting freshman essays, I'd felt a compelling urge to write to her and tell her that I loved her. The clear image of her lying in bed fighting her physical pain, minute by minute shrinking away from the battle, brought tears. I knew that she knew she was dying, and no matter how much others try to comfort you, that must be the most lonely of experiences, for any kind of death is a solitary event. Then it's really only you and the Lord who make up reality. And sometimes, because we're so human, we must claw very hard at the scales covering our own eyes to see his face clearly.

But I knew my aunt was all right. She was very brave and spiritual. Besides, I had to get those essays graded so that I could start revising the latter half of my thesis. It had to be written, approved of, and typed before my orals next month. I just didn't have time to write letters while trying to make all these deadlines before the new baby came. So I had smothered the impulse, feeling sure I'd be able to visit her soon and tell her in person. Then she died, not waiting for me, and I felt ashamed.

Mainly, I wanted to tell her thanks—thanks for believing in me so much. After I'd received a two-year associate degree from Ricks College, she'd called me to come and see her. I remember not wanting to go. I was depressed and I knew I'd find her cheerfully digging in her garden, and I didn't feel much like facing the positive mental attitude that flowed like air-conditioning through her house and yard. College, so far, had been an uphill fight, and I was tired. And money. College cost a lot of money, and the possibilities of continuing at BYU looked more than slim; though, of course, I was going to try.

True to form, my aunt shoved a piece of cake, a congratulations card, and a glass of punch in my hand, and chirped around her flowers until I couldn't help but forget my gloomy mood. Spring was spreading all over her yard, and she ripped and clawed through the dark earth in her garden like a miniature steam shovel, laughing and chattering and spraying the dog with clods.

But once back in the car, I let the gloom and self-pity descend again, and I felt powerless and small. Glancing down at the seat, I noticed her card, and at the next stoplight I picked it up to open it, at the same time thinking, *Nothing could possibly cheer me up except a fifty-dollar bill.* Then as I ripped the envelope open, a crisp new hundred-dollar bill fell out into my lap. I had to pull the car over, unable to drive for the tears. Of course, a hundred-dollar bill didn't pay for my education; it did more than that. It said to me that someone thinks that you are a hundred-dollar person, which seemed to give me enough self-esteem and energy to make it through a grueling summer work schedule.

Now as we walked behind the casket and the immediate family into the filled chapel, I narrowed my eyes so I would not have to recognize people. I didn't feel like smiling and nodding pleasantly. The flowers covering the pulpit and stand blended together into a pastel collage. Little five-year-old Sarah was sobbing uncontrollably, but more from tiredness and the somber looks of the adults around her than from anything else. The benches were hard, and as the first speaker read Aunt Theo's life history, the new baby curled up tight in my thick middle, then kicked viciously up under my ribs. And all at once I had to go to the bathroom again, for the third time in the last hour. *But bless its heart,* I thought. *I wonder what it looks like.*

The lady's voice droned on; my cousins sat quietly on the bench in front of us, and my mind began to wander along a familiar track. Lately I'd been imagining those quiet, early-morning hospital visits with the new baby. In my daydreams I'd hold the baby on my arm, fussing with the blanket, struggling with the beginning nursing procedure (nursing didn't come naturally for me, no matter how many books I read) until the baby fell asleep, which allowed me finally to study every eyelash and fingernail that was made carefully from my flesh. Then the baby was fully mine. I had paid for those few moments with nine months of nausea. I always dreamt of babies lately, fat wiggling babies.

Sarah stopped sobbing and fell asleep on her mother's lap. I spread my feet a little and leaned back against my husband's newly pressed dark suit, hoping no one would notice my hand massaging my side, trying to uncramp my muscles. It seemed almost sacrilegious to daydream about the birth of my baby at the funeral of my aunt. Birth, death, then birth again, bound up together. My aunt not dying, but maybe being born now. What was she doing at that precise moment? Where was she? Where was my sister Karon? Nothing ever ends. I knew they lived on, some place else. I didn't know for sure, but I wondered if they'd get to see the Savior in the flesh.

For moments I was filled with an intense aching to see him, too, and I tried to imagine his face and his body and his clothes and the expression in his eyes. Would I ever get to talk to him personally? What would I say? I guess I'd say I was sorry, and especially thanks. He'd been an unseen presence in my life for a long time now, even though I still didn't understand how he worked. In the temple ceremony, where there was much instruction, I absorbed only small amounts and knew that I comprehended even less. But I loved being there. Halfway through the session, my mind would give up trying so hard to figure things out, and I'd relax into the quiet dignity, listening to the cadence of the words, aware of my mind arranging itself into some sort of better pattern, aware of a higher presence.

The baby twisted again underneath my maternity dress, and my husband shifted his arm trying to make me more comfortable. I studied the flowers draping the coffin. Death is such a mystery—spiritual death, physical death. It's a cold thing, clammy like something foreign brushing your skin. I had read somewhere that "you cannot escape death except by dying."

I remembered talking to the bishop who brought me back into the Church in his quiet, cluttered office with the rain-spattered windows. The bishop had blessed me and said, "Someday you will kneel at the feet of the Savior and bathe his feet with tears of gratitude for the trials you've passed through." After I left his office I wondered about those words. How could anyone ever be thankful for suffering? Pain is pain, and there seems no way to get around that. Would we not all rather be happy? Yet as I unravel the threads of meaning running through each wrenching experience, each difficult adjustment, I see continuous evidence of the incredible power and mercy and compassion of God.

In front of me my uncle dropped his head, probably aware that soon even the coffin would be gone from him. But I noticed a slight smile on his face as he listened to the lady telling little anecdotes about my aunt. Waves of compassion washed through me for him, and along with them came waves of gratitude for my own life.

And who was I that God should have helped me so much? Just another Mormon girl who became lost for a while. Someone who knows nothing of either the mysteries or of the great wonders of life as yet, because she's had to spend so many years just crawling out of the pigsty she jumped into.

But this I know—that God lives and that he's good and that somehow I am related to him. Therefore, the possibilities of the future are infinite.

And as the funeral ended and we walked out into the March sunlight, a scripture from Alma ran through my mind: "I say, blessed be the name of my God, who has been mindful of us, wanderers in a strange land."